Manager's Guide to Virtual Teams

Other titles in the Briefcase Books series include:

To learn more about titles in the Briefcase Books series go to
www.briefcasebooks.com

Manager's Guide to Virtual Teams

Kimball Fisher and Mareen Fisher

McGraw-Hill

New York Chicago San Francisco Lisbon
London Madrid Mexico City Milan New Delhi
San Juan Seoul Singapore Sydney Toronto

The **McGraw·Hill** Companies

4 5 6 7 8 9 0 DOH/DOH 1 6 5 4

ISBN   978-0-07-175493-4
MHID   0-07-175493-8

This is a CWL Publishing Enterprises book developed for McGraw-Hill by CWL Publishing Enterprises, Inc., Madison, Wisconsin, www.cwlpub.com.

The publication is designed to provide accurate and authoritative information in regard to the subject matter covered. It is sold with the understanding that neither the author nor the publisher is engaged in rendering legal, accounting, futures/ securities trading, or other professional service. If legal advice or other expert assistance is required, the services of a competent professional person should be sought.
        —*From a Declaration of Principles Jointly Adopted by a*
            Committee of the American Bar Association and a Committee
            of Publishers and Associations

Library of Congress Cataloging-in-Publication Data

Product or brand names used this book may be trade names or trademarks. Where we believe there may be proprietary claims to such trade names or trademarks, the name has been used with an initial capital or it has been capitalized in the style used by the name claimant. Regardless of the capitalization used, all such names have been used in an editorial manner without any intent to convey endorsement of or other affiliation with the name claimant. Neither the author nor the publisher intends to express any judgment as to the validity or legal status of any such proprietary claims.

McGraw-Hill books are available at special quantity discounts to use as premiums and sales promotions, or for use in corporate training programs. For more information, please write to the Director of Special Sales, McGraw-Hill Professional, 1221 Avenue of the Americas, 45th Floor, New York, NY 10020. Or contact your local bookstore.

This book is printed on acid-free paper.

To our clients, who have always been our teachers and, thankfully, often our friends, as well.

Contents

Preface

We were thrilled to be invited by CWL Pubishing and McGraw-Hill to create *Manager's Guide to Virtual Teams* for the Briefcase Books series. This was an opportunity to revisit the material we published several years ago in *The Distance Manager*, also published by McGraw-Hill. We believe that the issues we discussed then are still important, perhaps even more important than they were at that time. Virtual teams have become common, and the challenges faced by virtual team managers are even more complex.

However, much has changed since the original book was published. At that time we lamented, for example, that no one had yet invented a combination of the PDA and the telephone so that we could manage e-mail, shared calendars, voice mail, and phone calls with one device. Now, smart phones are so common that it is hard to remember how we worked without them. Companies are using social networking techniques, blogging, and instant messaging that were unheard of when we originally published. But today's smart phones, Blackberries, and iPads will be replaced by technology we can't imagine, and in this book, we wanted to do something more than just respond to the latest wave of communication technology.

Many of the topics in *Manager's Guide to Virtual Teams* echo those we covered in our previous work, especially in the areas of trust building, the role of the virtual leader, employee expectations of leadership, focusing teams, and basic communication technology-use techniques. We cover new ground in chapters on managing performance from a distance, training virtual team members about their businesses and finance, engaging in team building, giving and receiving feedback, supporting group decision making, fostering problem solving, and what we believe has become an issue of extreme importance for managers of virtual teams, maintaining personal and work life balance in the age of intrusive technology.

Even when revisiting topics we have covered earlier, however, we've added more specific advice based on several more years of practical experience. Since we wrote *The Distance Manager*, we have had a busy consulting practice helping our clients apply these concepts; and although there is some common content, many of our current insights are different enough that we believed this new work was much needed. The unique approach of this series emphasizes pragmatism over theory, and promotes helpful tips over general observations. We like this practical approach, and we hope you find it helpful.

We want you to know that we are not just reporting the best practices of our wonderful *Fortune* 100 clients. We've used most of what we suggest at The Fisher Group, Inc. (www.thefishergroup.com), ourselves, because much of our work must be done virtually. As former managers, we've always been hesitant to recommend anything to a client that we wouldn't be willing to do in our own practice.

Special Features

The idea behind the books in the Briefcase series is to give you practical information written in a friendly person-to-person style. The chapters are short, deal with tactical issues, and include lots of examples. They also feature numerous sidebars designed to give you different types of specific information. Here's an overview of the types of sidebars and

KEY TERM

Every subject has some special jargon, including this one, dealing with virtual teams. These sidebars provide definitions of terms and concepts as they are introduced.

These sidebars do just what their name suggests: give you tips and tactics for using the ideas in this book to intelligently manage and encourage effective operations management practices in your organization.

Tricks of the Trade sidebars give you how-to hints on techniques astute managers use to execute the strategies and tactics described in this book.

It's always useful to have examples that show how the principles in the book are applied. These sidebars provide descriptions of how managers and organizations implement the techniques in this book.

Caution sidebars provide warnings for where things could go wrong in managing your virtual team and things you should be aware of to help prevent problems.

How can you make sure you won't make a mistake when you're trying to implement the techniques the book describes? You can't, but these sidebars will give you practial advice on how to minimize the possibility of an error.

This icon identifies sidebars where you'll find specific procedures, techniques, or technology you can use to successfully implement the book's principles and practices.

Acknowledgments

We wish to express our appreciation for the keen editorial insight of John Woods, who brought this project to us on behalf of Briefcase Books and our long time publishing partner, McGraw-Hill. Thanks also to our literary agent Mike Snell for his vigilant efforts on our behalf, and to our own company, The Fisher Group, Inc., for allowing us to use excerpts from The Distance Manager Training Program workbooks and assessments.

We give our most special thanks to our clients from whom we have learned much and to whom we dedicate this book. Without the virtual team leaders and team members at organizations like AXA Equitable, Apple Computers, CDW, Cummins Power Generation, DynoNobel, GE Capital, Hewlett-Packard, IBM, Microsoft, Nike Hong Kong, Ralston, State Farm Insurance, the U.S. Department of Treasury, the Staff Office of the U.S. Senate, and Weyerhaeuser, we wouldn't have much of practical value to share with our readers.

Kimball Fisher
Mareen Fisher
Portland, Oregon, USA

What Is a
Virtual Team?

Teamwork is the ability to work together toward a common vision
and the ability to direct individual accomplishment toward organizational objectives. It is the fuel that allows common people to attain
uncommon results.

—Andrew Carnegie

Let's consider three common situations involving virtual team management. Meeting challenges like those described here are part of what we discuss in this book.

Case One: The Global Team Management Challenge

Not too long ago we worked with a manager at Cummins Engine, Inc. He was located in the U.K., but the small teams reporting to him were scattered across more than twenty countries. An especially bright and capable leader, the manager found that he would seldom see a more significant challenge than coordinating the work of people sharing a common office. Leading global teams, for example, sometimes seemed like tiptoeing through an unmarked minefield. People had diverse cultural backgrounds and often interpreted the same e-mail in different (and sometimes contradictory) ways. Offense was taken when none was intended. Confusion and duplication of effort occurred with alarming regularity. Finding time for meetings that didn't conflict with someone's sleep schedule or national holiday was almost impossible. He was also concerned about the communication challenges associated with running an operation that required almost immediate access to him 24/7. How could he lead a balanced work and personal life when he was constantly tethered to work by his smartphone and computer?

Case Two: Can a Group of Remote Employees Really Function Like a Team?

A manager from IBM went through a significant downsizing in his organization, leaving him with 65 direct reports spread across the continental United States. Turnover was high enough that even with a grueling travel schedule, he could never meet all his direct reports in person before they transferred away. Unfortunately, temporary travel restrictions for nonmanagers made it impossible to get his team together in one place at the same time. All their meetings had to be Web meetings or teleconferences. But how could he help the team members get to know each other well enough to trust each other? Would they ever reach the comfort level that would allow them to openly admit mistakes, offer constructive criticism, share their best ideas, or ask each other for assistance? How could he help them—especially those who worked alone from their homes—overcome their inevitable feelings of isolation?

A team that shares a common office could get to know each other by taking breaks or having lunch together. Informal interaction in the hallways, at the water cooler, or in the parking lot builds relationships and a sense of common team identity. Celebrating birthdays and childbirths, sharing pictures of children and weddings, informally telling work stories about organizational disasters and victories and any of the thousand other tiny social interactions that connect people and create a social lubricant that facilitates working together would likely never happen. Was it even possible to create a highly functioning team in this situation?

Case Three: Can a Team That Shares a Common Office Be Virtual?

A manager of a sales team at the high-tech distribution giant CDW told us that she struggled with the challenges of managing people who were never in the office. Her sales team was almost always in the field working with customers. She was a good manager and had a track record of positive accomplishments, but many of her leadership practices were based on the traditional management model that assumed regular face-to-face interactions. She knew how to pop over a cubicle and help someone she could see was struggling with an assignment, how to gather an obviously confused group together for an emergency meeting, how to correct a misconception she overheard in the lunchroom, how to take full advantage of those fortunate moments when you run into someone in the hallway you need to speak with, or how to watch people and tell from their expressions and body language whether they understood or agreed with her.

When she observed gossiping, whining, blaming, or other behaviors she knew would erode the effectiveness of the team, she intervened immediately. If she saw cliques forming, behaviors that indicated disunity or silo thinking, or indications of the early stages of conflict brewing, she resolved them. She knew how to rally the troops when the tone of their comments indicated that they were discouraged. To continue the military analogy, she liked being on the frontlines, helping the wounded, and personally leading charges far into enemy territory. "But," she asked in an interview, "how do you lead a team over the Internet?" It felt to her like calling in orders to the battlefield when she was located in a tent, blinded and deafened by separation from her army, a million miles away.

The Challenges of Working with Virtual Teams

We have hundreds of these stories about the challenges of working with what are widely known as "virtual teams." They come from operations as diverse as large multinational insurance companies to the staff office of the U.S. Senate, and from jobs that range from Microsoft executives to Swedish R&D scientists in a mining explosives company. Even though these are very different organizations—both private and public, blue collar and white collar, large corporations and small home-based businesses—they share a common problem: How do you manage people you seldom see in person—especially when that group of people is supposed to be a cohesive and productive work team?

Why Are Virtual Teams Becoming So Common?

The bad news is that these types of operations are difficult to manage *and* they are increasingly common. Since the industrial revolution started more than a century ago, organizations have had employees who didn't work in the same location as their manager. But in the last several years, the number of these operations has exploded. Why? True global marketplaces have required that even smaller organizations have people closer to their customers, vendors, and key stakeholders.

Skilled workers now live everywhere instead of in clumps surrounding key corporations or schools. Employees who were once willing to relocate to wherever the employer needed them now have to manage multiple careers and are reluctant to move their kids. Businesses don't want to pay for relocation expenses. Cost pressures have also forced large organizations to reduce expensive brick-and-mortar office buildings and place key components of their businesses in other countries. The nature of work itself has changed from mostly physical labor to mostly knowledge work, allowing people to work away from farms, factories, and mines. (For more about this, see our book *The Distributed Mind*, Amacom, 1998.)

Perhaps most importantly, technology that allows people to do knowledge work jobs from anywhere is cheap, effective, and plentiful. The ubiquity of the Internet, in particular, allows people to coordinate their work regardless of location. What was once rare—a virtual team including employees who are remote from their manager and each other—is now commonplace. And it is unlikely that any professional manager will go through his or her entire career without having to manage at least one. Surprisingly, this is also the good news. These types of operations are increasingly common. That means that even though there are challenges, lots of people have already faced these challenges successfully.

There was a time when some experts wondered if an effective work team was even possible if its members weren't physically located together. They argued that communication technologies could never substitute for face-to-face interaction. We now know that is not true. Yes, it's more difficult to lead a group of people located all over the place. But it is possible. Lots of managers are doing it. In all three cases that open this chapter, for example, the leaders ended up not only solving their difficult problems, but excelling as virtual team managers.

Defining Virtual Teams

To begin our discussion, let's define *virtual teams*. Please note that there are many organizations that are not teams. If your operation doesn't require people to collaborate to achieve common goals, for instance, then a team structure isn't necessary. People can do independent work effectively even if they are isolated from each other. For example, we once worked with a utility that wanted to create teams, but when we helped management discover that individual gas meter readers didn't have to work with each other to accomplish their jobs, they quickly (and appropriately) abandoned the project. (Ironically, technology that now allows for the remote reading of meters makes the former nonteam of employees new candidates for teaming because they now have to collaborate to make the best use of the technology. Before, they could work in the field without sharing anything other than an occasional tip on how to deal with aggressive dogs.)

This book deals with virtual teams composed of people whose work depends on one another. We do not write about virtual *groups* of people. Unlike virtual groups, virtual *team* members have to collaborate to do their work, but unlike teams who are collocated, their mission is more difficult because they don't share a common office and/or work schedule.

> **Team** A group of people who share a common purpose and who must collaborate to get their work done.
>
> **Virtual team** People who must work together, but who can't frequently meet face-to-face because they:
>
> - Work in different locations
> - Work different time schedules

KEY TERMS

Virtual teams are more prevalent than many people believe. Our experience suggests you have a virtual team if *any* of the team members:

- Are located in different workplaces
- Work in shifts
- Travel frequently

- Often work from their homes, cars, or in the field
- Are assigned to multiple project teams
- Work part-time
- Report to more than one manager

If you're a student of virtual teams, you'll probably notice that our definition of virtual teams varies from that of some other experts in the field. Some, for example, consider virtual teams to be only those teams that are geographically dispersed. To them, a global team is obviously virtual, but a collocated 24-hour call center, 24/7 manufacturing plant or a multiple-shift IT help desk is not. But to us, the management dynamics of leading across a distance are similar whether the distance is geographic or is caused by working different hours. (For more on this, see our book *The Distance Manager*, McGraw-Hill, 2001).

One of the authors, for example, was a manager in a multiple-shift manufacturing plant operated by Procter & Gamble in Lima, Ohio. The plant continues to be one of the most advanced team-based operations in the world (described in detail in *Leading Self-Directed Work Teams*, McGraw-Hill, 2000). Because team members were scattered across three shifts, however, some people were always unavailable because they were home asleep. They might just as well have been living in a different state.

And although it is not part of our definition, we believe that culture is a third important variable affecting virtual teams. If team members are separated by significantly different cultures, they can be as behaviorally distanced from each other as if they were in a different country, regardless of whether they occupy the same space or time. This is especially obvious in those teams whose members may share a location but do not all speak the same language and therefore cannot collaborate effectively with each other. But it is also true when other cultural differences separate people and make it difficult for them to work together.

What's in This Book?

Now that we have defined virtual teams, we'd like to dedicate the rest of the book to helping you lead them more effectively. Common questions about managing virtual teams that we intend to answer in this book include:

- What are the major challenges of managing a virtual team?
- What is the leader's role?
- How do we help employees feel connected?
- How do we build trust from a distance?
- How do we communicate effectively?
- How should we use e-mail, teleconferences, instant messaging, and Web conferencing?
- How do we maintain relationships?
- What type of people should we hire to be on virtual teams?
- How do we orient new virtual team members?
- How do we manage across cultures?
- How do we manage the performance of people we can't see?
- How often should we get together in person?
- How do we maintain an effective team environment?
- How do we set up a virtual team?
- What are the practical tools needed to keep a virtual team focused and effective?
- How can we maintain a balanced work and personal life?
- How can we do virtual team building?

If you are interested in these questions, read on. In the next chapter we discuss why the three variables of space, time, and culture are so important to virtual teams, and we introduce the basic techniques for managing them.

Manager's Checklist for Chapter 1

☑ The three key variables that affect virtual teams are space, time, and culture. Each variable can create a sort of distance that effective virtual leaders need to bridge.

☑ A virtual team (1) is any group of people that has to collaborate to get its work done and (2) has members who work in different locations or during different hours.

☑ Virtual teams are increasingly common because global markets require them and cost-effective technologies now make them practical. Any serious manager needs to know how to manage them effectively.

☑ In this book we help you address the common challenges of virtual teams, and we share the best practices of excellent virtual leaders across the globe.

Chapter 2

Managing Space, Time, and Culture

Remember upon the conduct of each depends the fate of all.
—Alexander the Great

I n the last chapter we introduced the three key variables affecting virtual teams: space, time, and culture. In this chapter we explain why these variables are so important and suggest some steps you can take to address the challenges that come from a lack of shared offices and common working hours.

The Three Key Variables Affecting Virtual Teams

Why are these variables of space, time, and culture important? Team members located together (shared space) who work the same schedule (shared time) and know how to work together (shared culture) have a significant advantage over virtual teams. In this setting, for example, there are few obstacles to the formal and informal communication that are important for collaboration.

Team members can quickly and directly share project status, ideas, concerns, and questions, help each other learn their jobs, solve problems, and make joint decisions. Informally, they can run into each other in the hallways, see each other during breaks, or meet at lunch or in the parking lot. Not only does this interaction help with the socialization needs of team members (people will work and communicate more effectively with

SPACE, TIME, AND CULTURE

Managing the three key variables affecting virtual teams is critical. If you don't have shared physical space (collocation), create virtual space. If you don't have shared work hours (synchronous time), create virtual time. If you don't have a strong shared culture to guide team member behavior (homogeneity), then create a virtual culture. This book shows you how to do all three.

people they know than with strangers), but it also provides a serendipitous opportunity to coordinate and collaborate ("Hey Jane, I just heard that you're working on the X project. Can I ask you a couple of questions?"). Their shared culture helps them know what to do when they run into problems, have conflicts, or need to coordinate difficult assignments. Virtual teams seldom have these advantages of shared time, space, and culture, even though they must be able to compete with teams that do.

Space-Time

Obviously these three variables are strongly related and most virtual teams are affected by all three. Physicists tell us, for example, that space and time are actually part of the same continuum. This is easy to see if you imagine a widely dispersed team. If people are located in several places, then they will also be in different time zones. Thus, you could argue that as far as virtual teams are concerned, space-time is one variable rather than two.

Culture

Culture is also affected by space-time. The more distributed the team is in time and space, the more likely members are to have a fragmented (or what experts call a "heterogeneous") culture. Obviously, teams dispersed in several countries face challenges caused by geographic cultural differences. For example (and at the risk of perpetuating stereotypes), consider what some people have reported to us about working on global teams.

South Americans on a project may see timelines as approximate, while Germans may view them as precise, even though both sit through the same discussion in the same language at the same time. Asians may smile and nod their heads when asked to agree to something that they know they

---

TROUBLE IN SCANDANAVIA

A virtual new product development team of scientists at a Scandinavian company we worked with was having problems. Although they were some of the best and brightest technical minds in their field, coordination between the groups in Sweden and Norway and the group in the U.S. wasn't so effective, and the business suffered as a result. When the team got together to discuss delays in new product introductions, they discovered that one of the key problems was cultural.

Most of the Scandinavians took off the whole month of August for vacation, and the Americans resented it. The Swedes and Norwegians resented what they considered the unhealthy practice of American workaholism and the lack of respect for an important family and cultural tradition.

Once each side showed appropriate cultural sensitivity and understood the concerns of the other, however, they were able to compromise, and they put together a plan for vacation rotation and improved communication that allowed each group to meet most of its needs while making the required improvements to the business process.

---

cannot later support because the rudeness of overt disagreement is culturally intolerable. This behavior confuses their U.S. colleagues, who assume that nods and smiles mean agreement. North Americans may run roughshod over what they see as the unnecessary time-consuming practices of other cultures. This short-term efficiency focus may backfire in the long term as it erodes trust and employee commitment.

To add more complexity to this culture problem, Ed Schein, an M.I.T. professor whose research focused on organizational culture, has defined culture as *anything* that falls into the category of a "learned behavior about how to work together" (Edgar Schein, *Organizational Culture and Leadership*, 2nd Ed., Jossey-Bass, 1997). This definition appropriately allows for many things besides geography to influence the culture of a team, including organizational practices, educational backgrounds, and present and former leadership styles. Gaps in these areas can create a great deal of distance.

What Besides Geography Causes Cultural Distance?

In one company where we worked, the biggest and most divisive cultural difference wasn't based on location, but on organizational practices. Some recently acquired organizations had fragmented into warring fiefdoms.

CAUTION

CULTURE PROBLEMS

The most problematic cultural distance between team members is often caused by something other than nationality. Differences in education, organizational affiliation, or any personal life experiences can give rise to cultural misunderstandings and undermine effective teamwork. Managers need to keep this in mind when dealing with a team whose members have different cultural backgrounds (even if they all reside in the same geographic region).

Arguments were heated and common. Resources and information weren't shared. Cooperation and collaboration were rare. The company was concerned that unless the language (e.g., acronyms, business terminology), practices, processes, and attitudes of the acquired organizations became better aligned with the culture of the organization that had acquired them, the entire operation could fail.

We've heard similar concerns expressed about how the "culture" of a function such as engineering versus marketing or manufacturing can cause confusion and conflict in a team. For example, if a virtual project team composed of engineers, salespeople, and manufacturing people can't get their job done because they don't understand or respect each other, is that any less problematic than if the root of their conflict comes from geographic cultural differences?

We've been in many teams where the engineers have complained about the lack of technical savvy of the manufacturing people and wondered why the salespeople don't sell the products they have instead of pestering engineering for changes. The manufacturing people have complained that the engineers are too theoretical and don't design for the real world. They think salespeople are naive and have no idea about how unrealistic schedules affect a factory. The salespeople lament the realities of the market and can't comprehend the unwillingness of engineering and manufacturing to address customer needs. Ironically, we have watched people transfer from one function to the other, soon forgetting their previous concerns and taking on the speech patterns and sympathies of the new functional culture they had joined. It's like watching someone move to another country, learn its language and habits, and eventually abandon all traces of the former life.

In a team with many geographic cultures, there can be difficult problems around questions like "What do certain words or gestures mean?" or "How do we make sure we understand each other?" or "How can people with significantly differently viewpoints collaborate?" If they go unresolved, the team cannot perform at the highest level. But smart virtual team leaders realize that these questions can be just as problematic

SHARED CULTURES CAN BE DYSFUNCTIONAL
CAUTION

Just because you have a homogeneous (shared) culture doesn't mean the team can't improve. Some strong, shared cultures can create "groupthink," a consistency in approach and thinking that limits creativity and innovation. More importantly, a common culture may actually have to be modified if it becomes dysfunctional. In this case it becomes more dangerous than a fragmented culture because it is more likely to cause behavioral problems across the entire team.

when the cultural difference stems from personal life experiences related to education, organizational affiliation, religion, gender, sexual orientation, race, socioeconomic circumstances, disability, military experience, or a whole host of other factors.

DEALING WITH CULTURAL DIFFERENCES
SMART

Determine what kind of cultural issues are affecting your team. Are they rooted in organizational differences, country-of-origin differences, technical discipline differences, a combination of several of these, or something else? Treat the situation appropriately. For example, technical training may be required to bridge the chasm caused by technical discipline differences in approaching problems or making decisions.

MANAGING

On the other hand, if the differences spring from organizational cultures, discussion and compromise may be the key. Serious culture differences of any type may require special training in cross-cultural sensitivity. In some cases professional consultation or mediation may be required. This help is especially important when it concerns issues that may have legal consequences.

Use Whatever Advantages You Have

We devote most of the rest of this book to a discussion of how to create virtual time, space, and culture for those teams that do not have the benefit of sharing either a common office or common work hours. But if your virtual team has the advantage of sharing space or time, we'd first like to discuss ways to use these opportunities.

Using Shared Space

Some virtual teams, such as a single-location 24-hour call center or factory, have multiple shifts of employees on the same team. They can't normally get everybody together at the same time, but they do have everybody work in the same location at different times. If you have the advantage of sharing a common space, use it. Create a physical place that provides a sense of identity and a means for collaboration. Carve out a place for a team room where people can cluster and talk when they have overlapping schedules. Some organizations, for example, designate certain areas as gathering and meeting places. These rooms normally have a whiteboard and comfortable chairs surrounding a table. They are spaces that encourage people to share ideas with each other, solve problems, and collaborate.

Decorate the team space with identity-enhancing graphics. For example, these teams often benefit from posters, charts, and graphs located on the walls. Post your goals, project timelines, or other key measures in places where they are visible to everyone. These types of community report cards can be updated each shift to obtain high-quality data, but more important, they are a visible reminder that each shift is part of a team that transcends its time period. Some teams—like the original Macintosh team at Apple Computers who flew a Skull and Crossbones flag over their building—create a symbol they use to reinforce their shared identity with people who work at other times.

Most operations of this type find that they have to create shift overlap in the schedule to accommodate and encourage team communication. This is easier in operations using eight-hour shifts than in organizations using twelve-hour shifts, but it is always preferable to create the opportunity for face-to-face interchange whenever possible. During the overlap, most organizations have some sort of shift download meeting where incoming team members find out what happened on the last shift. This time is always scarce and should be used efficiently for the activities that are best done face-to-face. If a team decision is to be made, for example, some of the suggestions might be gathered asynchronously on the team

Web site at the convenience of the team members throughout the shifts. The meeting time may then be reserved to discuss the pros and cons of each suggestion.

Using Shared Time

Some virtual teams have people in several locations, but they still have some regular overlap in daily work schedules. Use what you have. Most of these teams find it useful to have regularly scheduled conference meetings during the time overlap in the same way that collocated teams have staff meetings. The most common frequency for these virtual conferences is weekly, although many of these types of teams find that a brief daily meeting is helpful to coordinate assignments.

Some virtual teams are located in a sufficiently small geography that face to face meetings can be held without incurring significant travel expenses. It is good practice to have these with sufficient frequency that team members can have most of the advantages of a collocated team. For this type of team, a quarterly meeting at a central location should not be difficult. Increased frequency is recommended if team members can benefit from sharing ideas, coordinating with others, or participating in joint problem solving or decision making.

Remember to save the face-to-face meetings for things that aren't easily accomplished through virtual interactions. You might keep a running agenda for the meetings that anyone can contribute to (perhaps a space on your Web site titled "Topics for upcoming face-to-face meetings"). This way, you can schedule a meeting as soon as you have a sufficient agenda to justify one.

What If You Share Neither Time nor Space?

Teams with no (or severely limited) shared time or space need a way to coordinate the day-to-day work through a variety of collaboration technologies. Coordinating the timing of synchronous meetings can be a headache in these teams because some members are almost always required to participate at a bad time for them (middle of their night, holidays, weekends, etc.). We have a business contact in Moscow, for example, who has an 11-hour time difference from our location in Portland, Oregon. Every virtual meeting requires someone to work outside of the "normal" 8 A.M. to 5 P.M. workday. In these cases, do your best to minimize this problem by choosing the least disruptive times. Rotate meeting times so that the same people aren't always inconvenienced.

In many cases virtual interaction still isn't enough for people who share neither time nor space. Do something that allows people to get together in person, as well. The frequency of these interactions depends on your situation. These types of virtual teams range from never having a face-to-face meeting to having one every other week. In our experience, the most common frequency is a quarterly meeting that focuses on the things best done in person, including some social activities (dinner, golf, etc.) that facilitate team building. Avoid concerts, movies, or other activities that won't allow people to interact with one other.

Finally, find a way to create some team space. Some virtual teams at Hewlett-Packard, for example, actually set up desks for the offsite team members in the office where most team members are located. This isn't practical or cost effective in most situations, but where teaming is critical, HP finds that this makes the offsite employees feel more like full partners than periodic associates.

At a minimum, set up a team wiki or Web site to be a virtual space for your team. This will help create a shared identity for team members and help them feel less isolated. Include a "virtual water cooler" section on the site—a place where people can hang around and share the tacit information that keeps an organization going. For example, many teams have a chat room space on their intranet or team Wiki that allows more informal virtual interaction asynchronously. Team members from one shift can also leave notes to the next shift on the space, maintaining a type of ongoing operational log to capture important information and concerns.

A certain portion of the site should be designed by the team members themselves to allow them to get to know each other better. Many teams include their photos, videos, or links to personal social networking pages from sites like Facebook or LinkedIn.

Manager's Checklist for Chapter 2

☑ There are different types of virtual teams depending on how the three key variables of space, time, and culture affect them. Use whatever advantages you can on your team. If you share a common space, use it to help overcome challenges with communication and team identification. If you have some common time (even if it's only a brief overlap in the morning or evening), use it to discuss the highest-priority issues of the team synchronously. If you have a common culture (and it's functional), use it to align and motivate the team.

☑ If you don't have common space, time, or culture on your team, you need to create virtual space, time, and culture. The rest of this book tells you how.

☑ A lot of things that can cause cultural difficulties on a virtual team. Conflicting cultures can be created by differences in country of origin, education, organization, or life experience. And even if you have a common culture on your team, it might not be a good thing. A common but dysfunctional culture, for example, can be more counterproductive than a fragmented one.

Note

Much of the discussion about the three variables affecting virtual teams comes from our book *The Distance Manager* (McGraw-Hill, 2001) and our Assessment Tool, *Assessing Virtual Teams* (The Fisher Group, Inc., 2010). Used by permission of authors and copyright holders. Some of the information about culture first appeared in a chapter Kimball wrote for *The Handbook of High-Performance Virtual Teams* (edited by Nemiro et al., Jossey-Bass, 2008) entitled "Tools for Effective Virtual Team Start-Ups." Used by permission of the author.

The Seven Competencies of Effective Virtual Team Leaders

If your actions inspire others to dream more, learn more, do more, and become more, you are a leader.

—John Quincy Adams

We have spent almost three decades trying to understand how to make leaders more effective, first in our own management jobs at Procter & Gamble, Tektronix, and Weyerhaeuser, and later as consultants to about one-quarter of the *Fortune* 100 companies (such as Apple Computers, Bristol-Myers Squibb, Capital One, Chevron, Intel, McDonald's, Microsoft, NBC [General Electric], Toyota, and Tropicana [PepsiCo]).

What is obvious to us (and, we suspect, every other serious manager in the world) is that there are certain fundamental practices necessary for all leaders regardless of title, level, or responsibility.

These practices include things like being appropriately proactive, being an excellent communicator, and developing people effectively. Thankfully—especially given the sad and very public recent history of large business failures across the globe—there is also emerging agreement on a new, higher standard of ethics and transparency in leadership. One of our friends, for example, who recently attended his son's graduation from the Harvard Business School, remarked that he was pleased to see that MBAs are now "strongly encouraged to stay out of jail."

But we have come to believe there are certain practices and perspectives *especially* important for leaders of virtual teams. To that end, in this chapter we describe the seven competencies we think are essential. This information comes from hundreds of interviews we have conducted with managers over the years as we have asked them the question, "What do effective virtual team leaders do?"

The Seven Competencies of Virtual Team Leaders

To share what we have learned from recent interviews, we have revised a model of virtual team leadership we wrote about in our first book on the topic (*The Distance Manager*, McGraw-Hill, 2001). As shown in Figure 3-1, these seven key competencies are *leader, results catalyst, facilitator, barrier buster, business analyzer, coach,* and *living example.* In this chapter, we describe each of these competencies and explain each one's importance to virtual team managers. We start with the core competency (leader) and then go to results catalyst and work our way around the model counterclockwise, ending with living example.

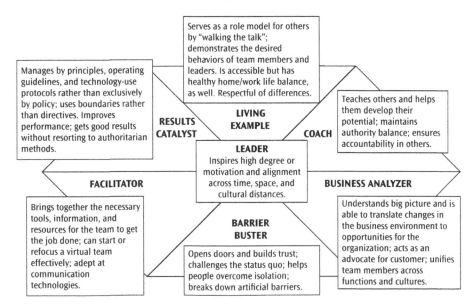

Figure 3-1. The seven competencies of effective virtual team leaders

Leader

Not surprisingly, being a *leader* is the core competency for effective virtual team leadership. What does that mean? Of course it includes some of the things you would expect in a discussion about leadership. Being a leader, for example, is different from being a manager (see Figure 3-2).

Leadership	Management
■ Inspires others to do their best work·	■ Instructs others in specific work methods
■ Helps others make good decisions	■ Asks others to implement decisions and resolutions that have been made for them
■ Helps others solve problems effectively	
■ Motivates people through a vision of a desirable future	■ Asks people to comply with rules and regulations
■ Focuses on ends (results, profitability)	■ Focuses on means (procedures, etc.)
■ Favors educational processes	■ Favors disciplinary processes
■ Shares information widely	■ Shares information as need-to-know
■ Is skilled at teaching others how to plan, organize, direct, and control	■ Is skilled at planning, organizing, directing, and controlling
■ Emphasizes strategy	■ Emphasizes tactics
■ Uses effectiveness as key measure	■ Uses efficiency as key measure

Figure 3-2. Leadership versus management

Although the various administrative skills like planning, organizing, directing, and follow-up (normally associated with effective management competencies) are essential on a virtual team, the managers we interviewed strongly suggested that most of that work has to be done by the team itself. If these teams aren't effectively "self-organizing," they argued, then virtual team leaders are dead in the water.

When a virtual team leader emphasizes management over leadership, he or she will normally create dependence instead of independence, compliance instead of creativity and innovation, and rigidity instead of flexibility and responsiveness. Virtual team members chafe under what they view as efforts to micromanage their work, and they wonder why

> **Self-organizing teams** This term is synonymous with *self-directed work teams*. Both terms refer to teams with a high degree of worker empowerment and minimal supervision.
> **KEY TERM** While it is often optional for collocated teams to be self-organizing, virtual teams normally need to be self-organizing because increased supervision is not an option. That doesn't mean, of course, that all virtual teams are good at being self-organizing, nor that all virtual team leaders are good at empowering their teams. An enormous amount of work is required by managers to help teams learn how to effectively manage themselves during the frequent absences of the formal leader.
>
> For more about how to deal with this difficult dilemma, see our book *Leading Self-Directed Work Teams*. Most of our clients prefer to use the term *high-performance work teams* to refer to these types of operations. We also like this term because it emphasizes the result of the team (ends) over the method used to obtain the result (means). Helping virtual team members understand this distinction is an important part of the leadership role. There is little value to empowered autonomy unless it results in improved organizational returns.

someone who doesn't see them often could possibly be more competent at doing it than they can. See the next chapter about employee expectations for more on this topic.

A virtual team leader can't see what team members are doing and has to rely on them to be self-starters. If team members wait to be directed by a distant leader, productivity will die, and the team (along with the manager) will not succeed. These managers have to be able to trust their peo-

> **SMART**
> ## Do It **With** Them, Not **For** Them
> **MANAGING** Virtual team managers often manage people instead of leading them because it's easier. When a frustrated virtual team member comes to you with a problem or complaint, it's often easier to solve the problem yourself than to help the person learn how to solve it. But as the famous Taoist saying goes, "If you give a man a fish you feed him for a day. If you teach him how to fish you feed him for a lifetime." If you keep doling out fish, you create dependence. You can't afford to have team members calling you with every difficulty. So when team members call with a customer problem, a technical breakdown, or a disagreement with a fellow team member they want you to fix, consider doing it *with* them, not *for* them. It takes more effort, but it will show them how to do it without you next time.

ple, to count on them meeting commitments, and to know that they will ask for help if it's needed. Thus, although management skills are necessary, the manager normally teaches these management techniques to team members, rather than employing them herself or himself.

"OK," we said, "so what do you mean by *leadership*?" The leaders we talked to answered with many of the things you would expect, such as inspiring people to do their best and using vision as a tool of alignment.

But they also confirmed that there are certain areas where these efforts are crucial on virtual teams, especially skills for dealing with people across the distance of space, time, and culture. Giving a presentation virtually, for example, is a different experience from doing it face-to-face. Even more critical are the skills associated with delivering performance feedback to someone you can't see, or intervening to change a dysfunctional team culture during a Web meeting or

> **Vision** A verbal picture of the possible future direction of an organization. **KEY TERM** Consider some examples from the public sector. A simple but well-crafted vision such as John F. Kennedy's "We will place a man on the moon" or Ronald Reagan's "Tear down that wall" or Mahatma Gandhi's "nonviolent change" or Mikhail Gorbachev's "*perestroika*" can inspire incredible motivation and action. Martin Luther King's famous "I have a dream" speech is an excellent example of a vision stated in a way that provides clarity of direction and provokes institutional change.

VISION BLOGGING

One of the powerful tools for a leader is a personal vision of greatness for his or her team. How does the leader communicate this vision? Some leaders we've worked with keep a blog on their team Web page to share elements of their vision and reinforce it with current examples. If your vision includes something like reducing your team's carbon footprint, for example, periodically note in your blog how Maya in the Alberta office found a way to reduce the need to travel through better use of Web conferencing or Giles in Manchester figured out how to conserve power in his home office. Or if your vision includes cost containment, share that story about how Lacey in the San Jose office negotiated a lower cost for expensive office supplies. You'll be rewarding good performance publicly, sharing best practices, and reinforcing your vision all at the same time.

teleconference. And almost to a person, these managers insisted that a virtual team leader has to be especially sensitive to cultural issues. An inappropriate joke, unintended violation of important norms, or unskillful treatment of an individual's cultural concern about another team member can destroy a virtual team.

Results Catalyst

The second competency is *results catalyst*. Virtual team managers know that inspiring and motivating from a distance is important, but unless it produces bottom-line results, it is insufficient. The managers we interviewed also reported that it was not just getting results that was critical, but getting them in a certain way.

For example, instead of getting results from dictates and controls or other authoritarian methods, they preferred to use more facilitative and developmental approaches such as a technique we call *boundary conditions* (see Figure 3-3). These methods, they reported, generate a feeling of personal empowerment and are more likely to produce sustainable results. Moreover, they don't create an overreliance on the remote manager who may not be available at critical times when employees have to make quick decisions to save money, be responsive to customers, or avoid work delays.

Directives	Boundary Conditions
Specifies what needs to be done and how it should be accomplished	Specifies the constraints and limitations that must be considered before the group determines what is to be done and how it can be accomplished
Management Driven	Shared Leadership

Adapted from the Leadership Skills training program, The Fisher Group, Inc. © 2010. All rights reserved. Used with permission.

Figure 3-3. Directives vs. boundary conditions

It is far easier to focus on the tasks at hand than the results that must be achieved, but a results catalyst knows this is a dangerous mistake. Many an organization has suffered when a function, for example, completed an assignment, but did it in a way that created more harm than good. There is a good reason that physicians subscribe to the Hippocratic

> **Boundary conditions** These reveal restrictions and constraints (such as budgets, deadlines, or laws) that must be considered when making decisions. When a leader shares the boundaries within which a decision must be made, he or she is empower- **KEY TERM** ing the employee to make the decision in a way that is more likely for the process to be successful. For example, an effective virtual team manager would normally say, "Juan, why don't you decide what to do for the next step of this project. Just remember that we can't spend more than $2K and that it has to be cleared with engineering," rather than "Please do such and such." Why? Because if Juan makes the decision himself (appropriately considering the boundary conditions), he'll "own" it. That means he'll make sure it is implemented properly, he'll fix it if it doesn't work, and the results will be better than if he feels he is simply executing someone else's orders.

Oath to "do no harm," because it is possible to cure a disease but kill a patient in the process. Many organizations find themselves unwittingly doing the same thing. A seemingly innocuous decision to shortcut an environmental process, save money on preventive maintenance activities, or save time and effort by ignoring small warning signs of potential people, political, or equipment problems could have disastrous results. One organization we worked with got so caught up in completing an interesting management information project that although they produced an award-winning, state-of-the-art management reporting system, they spent so much money on it that they had to increase the prices of their services, losing customers as a result.

Facilitator

The third competency is *facilitator*, the role of providing appropriate resources for the team to do its work. These resources include things like budgets, personnel, tools, training, and information. One of the most important things facilitators do for virtual teams is ensure that team meetings are effective. This is a key resource for effective team coordination, decision making, and problem solving. In a virtual team, much of this has to be done via technology.

Managers must be highly skilled, for example, at facilitating Web meetings—a skill set that requires more than face-to-face facilitation techniques. This also requires that virtual team leaders be proficient in communicating via tools like e-mail, instant messaging, and teleconfer-

---

TRICKS OF THE TRADE

COMMUNICATING WITH PEOPLE YOU CAN'T SEE

Why is it a problem to communicate with someone you can't see? Because humans are hardwired to use visual cues like body language, facial expressions, and gestures to facilitate communication. So what do you do if you can't see these visual cues? Some teams at Hewlett Packard use visual imagery in teleconferences. They might say, "Martha, are you frowning right now?" or "Alex, I bet you're shaking your head" to draw people into fuller and more effective conversations.

Managers also have to remember to ask if people have questions because they can't see a confused expression over the telephone or e-mail. And it's always a good idea to confirm any decision by having the people responsible for implementing that decision repeat back what they are going to do. This is a good double-check of the effectiveness of the communication. Don't ask them if they understand what you said. In some cultures it's rude to say no, even if they didn't understand a single thing.

---

encing. Experienced managers know that this isn't as easy as it sounds. How do you convey appropriate emotion (excitement, sadness, etc.) over e-mail? How do you make sure that a communication is written in a way that doesn't unintentionally convey the wrong message or leave things too open to interpretation? At the time of this writing, communication vehicles with a video component are still not always available, and managers must therefore also be proficient in communicating with someone, or with a collection of several people, whom they cannot see.

Barrier Buster

The fourth competency is *barrier buster*. This is the ability to remove those obstacles that get in the way of the highest possible performance from employees individually and collectively. In a collocated facility, these barriers—things like conflict, organizational structures and policies, or even low self-esteem—are often glaringly visible. But in a virtual team, these barriers are more likely to be kicked under the rug and ignored. This isn't good! Assume that barriers always exist and actively ferret them out. Regularly ask, "What prevents you from reaching your highest level of performance?" to individuals in one-on-one teleconferences and to the team as a whole in Web conferences. Always be working to eliminate the policies, structures, conflicts, or other problems that get in the way of producing the best organizational results.

Business Analyzer

Think of the next competency, *business analyzer*, as the ability to manage businesses instead of functions or sites (the skills associated with managing the whole instead of just its parts). It's important that a virtual team leader, for example, be sensitive to whether team members feel isolated or disconnected from the team or business, and that he or she intervenes appropriately to do virtual team-building activities when the need arises.

These interventions may even require the leader to work with other teams across the organization to ensure that the business, not just his or her part of it, is successful. It may require working with customers, government compliance agencies, or other stakeholder groups in the business environment.

One special emphasis here is the area of culture development. "Often," one manager said, "the culture that gets established in a virtual team has to be improved. It is easy for the team to fall into habits of being noncommunicative, being disrespectful of others, or not being accountable. If the leader doesn't intervene, the team results will eventually suffer."

> **MAKE IT GOOD FOR ALL**
>
> **FOR EXAMPLE**
>
> A good business analyzer understands that what is best for his or her operation may not be best for the organization as a whole. We worked in one operation, for example, where the procurement team was proud of the fact that it had saved tens of thousands of dollars on contracts through tough negotiations with vendors.
>
> Unfortunately, vendors consequently decreased their quality to a point that more than a million dollars of final product had to be recalled from customers because the substandard components of the vendors failed in the field. It was a classic tale of suboptimization (optimizing a part of the organization to the detriment of the whole).

We recommend early intervention. As we frequently suggest, all problems are magnified by distance. If you think something might be a problem, it usually is. If you think it's a small problem, it's probably huge. And if you think it's a big problem, it might already be too late to fix. This topic is important enough that we dedicate an entire chapter to it later in the book.

Coach

In terms of time, the sixth competency, *coach*, probably consumes more of the virtual team leader's workday than any other. Virtual teams need a lot of coaching to be successful. This includes coaching and training in technical, interpersonal, and business skills both for individuals and for the team as a whole. And it takes a lot of time just to determine the areas where the coaching is needed. In later chapters we discuss how to improve performance from a distance and cover this issue in detail.

KEY TERM **Coaching** A series of interventions a manager makes to improve team performance. Like the sports metaphor suggests, coaches recruit, help team members acquire and apply skills, help them work effectively as both individuals and teams, and help them learn from mistakes and get better and better results (win games).

Whenever a manager is giving feedback on performance, helping a team member put together a plan to acquire new skills (through schooling, training, new project assignments, mentoring, etc.), doing a performance appraisal, providing team or individual training, or conducting a postmortem on a project to see what improvements could be made next time, he or she is coaching.

Living Example

The final competency is *living example*. Virtual team managers must set an example for how they expect others on the team to behave. In today's business environment, employees are skeptical about management. They believe in actions, not words; personal examples, not policies; and they believe in budgets, not in stated intentions about where resources will eventually be applied. They expect that their leaders will set an example about things like effective communication, personal responsibility, and good meeting management.

We read not too long ago, for example, about a high school principal in the Portland, Oregon, area who retired and then volunteered her services for free for the next school year in order to avoid laying off two other teachers. It's one thing to say you'll fight for more teachers, but another thing altogether to volunteer a year of your own personal life. One of our favorite stories about a virtual team leader being a living example comes from a then-subsidiary of Tektronix.

A manager in the Grass Valley Group had a number of people on his team who traveled extensively. One day he had to assign a team member who had just returned from a trip to get on an airplane over the weekend to deal with yet another customer emergency. The team member complained that he hadn't even had time to mow his lawn due to his grueling schedule. The manager knew that the concern was well justified. But he didn't just express empathy and encouragement as many team leaders might have, he took his son over to the employee's house that Saturday to mow the lawn.

Did that require a personal sacrifice? Yes. But it left a lasting impression on the employee (who is the coworker of a friend who told us this story). A lecture about how sometimes we have to sacrifice for the good of the company can be useful, but a demonstration by a living example carries a lot more impact. And it said more about how that leader cared about his team than an expression of appreciation in a meeting ever could.

How Do I Determine My Effectiveness as a Virtual Team Leader?

Ultimately, the answer to the question "Am I a good virtual team leader?" is determined by the results of the team(s) you lead. Good managers get good results. But to determine whether you are applying the best practices of effective virtual team leaders, consider completing an assessment like the one below.

Distance Manager Effectiveness Assessment

Instructions: Assess your effectiveness as a virtual team manager by considering how often the following questions are true in your management practice (Always, Frequently, Sometimes, or Never). Statements that receive lower than a "Frequently" rating may indicate an opportunity for improvement.

Leader

1. Helps the virtual team understand exactly what it is responsible for.
2. Responds to communication (e-mails, voice mails, etc.) from team members within 24 hours.

3. Empowers the team by ensuring they have the authority, resources, information, and accountability to be successful.
4. Provides effective "start-up" or "refocusing" interventions for virtual teams, including a face-to-face meeting of all members on a regular basis.
5. Ensures that effective information-sharing, problem-solving, and decision-making processes are in place.
6. Manages by sharing information/data, not by asking people to conform to unnecessary rules and regulations.

Results Catalyst

7. Focuses on results.
8. Clearly states the limits (boundary conditions) within which the team can make decisions.
9. Actively supports team decisions that are within stated boundary conditions.
10. Strives to manage by a set of guiding principles (i.e., core guiding beliefs) rather than by policy only.
11. Makes sure the team establishes and uses a set of operating guidelines.
12. Establishes clear performance goals and metrics set jointly with the team and discussed regularly.

Facilitator

13. Models good team meeting preparation and facilitation.
14. Helps the team understand and use effective decision-making processes.
15. Is sensitive to group dynamics and deals effectively with dysfunctional behaviors.
16. Helps the team solve technical problems; ensures the understanding and use of appropriate problem-solving tools.
17. Helps the team solve people problems; ensures the understanding and use of appropriate problem-solving tools.
18. Helps the team solve business problems; ensures the understanding and use of appropriate problem-solving tools.

Barrier Buster

19. Works actively to remove unnecessary policies, procedures, or work practices that hinder team performance.
20. Corrects differences between what the company says it wants to have people do and what it actually rewards people for doing.
21. Actively works with individual team members to help them overcome feelings of isolation.
22. Helps the team understand, recognize, and manage different kinds of conflict.
23. Recognizes when he or she is a barrier to the team and takes necessary improvement action.

Business Analyzer

24. Communicates information about what is happening in other parts of the organization.
25. Discusses specific data about product/service performance with the team on a frequent basis.
26. Frequently discusses specific data about competitors with the team.
27. Discusses specific data about financial performance with the team on a frequent basis.
28. Ensures that team members know how to use communication technology effectively.
29. Acts like serving the customer is the most important priority.

Coach

30. Transfers responsibility and builds problem-solving skills in others by asking questions rather than always giving answers.
31. Ensures that members of the the team have effective ways to communicate with each other.
32. Allocates time and money for training and development activities.
33. Deals with poor performance appropriately.
34. Exhibits good feedback skills and teaches these skills to team members.
35. Ensures that the team develops and uses appropriate technology protocols (agreements on how to use e-mail, voice mail, Web conferences, etc.).

Living Example

36. Provides a personal example of the way people act in a virtual team setting.
37. Admits mistakes freely and openly.
38. Follows through on agreements.
39. Is willing to do things that are personally inconvenient if it helps the team.
40. Will do what he or she thinks is right even if it may be disruptive to personal career goals.
41. Behaves consistently with corporate values and ethics.

Remember that a self-assessment only provides your point of view. The most accurate way to complete an assessment of your management skill is to gather data from those you lead.

A periodic assessment of your effectiveness as a virtual team leader is a good way to provide the opportunity for feedback, personal development, and organizational improvement. Our experience indicates that leadership effectiveness is the single most important variable associated with virtual team success.

Manager's Checklist for Chapter 3

☑ Critical skills for virtual team leaders include things like helping team members become self-sufficient, communicating effectively over technology, managing performance from a distance, dealing effectively with multiple cultures, helping their team improve its culture when necessary, training team members in technical, interpersonal, and business skills, eliminating barriers to performance, and setting a personal example of how to act on a virtual team.

☑ The seven competencies for effective virtual team leaders include: leader, results catalyst, facilitator, barrier buster, business analyzer, coach, and living example.

☑ A Leader inspires and motivates through vision, not management techniques.

☑ The results catalyst helps the team stay focused on getting good results.

☑ The facilitator gets the team the resources it needs and helps the team members interact as effectively as possible.

☑ The barrier buster eliminates impediments to increased performance.

☑ The business analyzer optimizes the whole of the business rather than just the team he or she leads.

☑ The coach works to improve both individual and organizational performance.

☑ The living example provides a personal role model of organizational values and ethics.

Note

An earlier version of the "Seven Competencies of the Virtual Team Manager" was published in *The Distance Manager* (McGraw-Hill, 2001). The questions for the "Distance Manager Effectiveness Assessment" are a sampling of our assessment tool of the same name (The Fisher Group, Inc., 2010) and are used by permission of the authors and copyright holders.

What Virtual Team Employees Need from Their Manager

Most of what we call management consists of making it difficult for people to get their work done.

—Peter Drucker

We would like to share a personal (and somewhat embarrassing) example of how easy it is to make mistakes as virtual team managers. A few years ago we experienced some challenges associated with shipping and retrieving training materials to and from some of our clients. Our team is composed of consultants (who are normally on the road and/or located in other states from our corporate office in Oregon) and customer service and materials coordinators (who are located at the corporate office). As company leaders we immediately diagnosed the problem and created a thorough tracking system that we created. This gave us the confidence that things were under control when we and the other consultants were on the road.

Once we instructed the materials coordinator how to implement the solution, we assumed it was fixed. Not long afterward, however, the problem resurfaced, and materials shipped to another client site were somehow misplaced. Frustrated, we called a special team meeting to resolve the problem before it affected other clients. During the meeting, we realized that we had used the very approach we cautioned our clients against. For some time we had recommended that managers "share the problem, not the solution" as a way to empower others. But instead, we had only shared our solution and asked people to implement it. We controlled the people (by conferring blame and demanding that our idea be implemented) instead of the process (discussing our ideas with others and focusing on the tools and techniques necessary for fixing the problem).

We apologized for mandating a solution and began to control the process instead. We described the problem and invited the materials coordinator to develop a new work process of her choosing that would solve it. The coordinator created a new, less cumbersome tracking system that did just that. The problem went away, and the coordinator felt that she had been empowered to solve it. Where before she had just been implementing someone else's solution, she now had a feeling of ownership for implementing and maintaining her own solution to the problem (which we discovered in the discussion, by the way, was more due to *our* lack of communication than to the material coordinator's lack of attention to detail as we had assumed).

We discovered how easy it is to slip back into controlling the person instead of managing the machines, techniques, or series of steps necessary to accomplish the work. Our new mantra at work is "We need a better process" instead of "Who made the mistake?" As a consequence, virtual team members have created work processes that range from an accountability system to make sure that assignments are followed up on to a new process for licensing our materials. These work processes provide direction and focus for the work whether we are on site or not.

How Do You Control Distance Workers?

"My biggest concern," confided one virtual team leader, "is that they won't be productive when I'm not there. How do you control offsite employees?" The saying goes, "When the cat's away, the mice will play." This has been quoted to us many times by concerned managers. We are also embarrassed to confess that we have sometimes felt this ourselves.

As our story at the start of the chapter demonstrates, however, it may be this very way of thinking that lessens the leader's ability to maintain appropriate control of an offsite workforce. Thinking that workers need to be controlled often causes the distance leader to over-control through policies and procedures that can actually cause the problem the leader so assiduously wants to avoid.

What Do Virtual Team Members Need from Their Leaders?

If you ask team members what they want from a virtual team manager, you seldom hear them ask for more autoc-

> ### THE PROBLEM WITH CONTROL
> **FOR EXAMPLE**
>
> Remote workers often feel distrusted or inadequate if their work environment is based on hierarchically generated control. This negatively affects their work. When workers feel overcontrolled by management, he or she tends to act in one of the following ways: (1) They become compliant and dependent on the manager, (2) they resist the controls and find ways to play games to get around them, or (3) they become apathetic. None of these states promotes the highest level of employee performance.

racy, hierarchy, or bureaucracy. More clarity, yes; definite priorities, sure; a sense of direction, absolutely. But more than the traditional management attributes of planning, organizing, directing, and controlling, team members want the sort of coaching and facilitation that comes from someone who sees his or her job as supporting rather than directing the team. They probably want the same things from you that you want from your leader.

Specifically, we consistently hear team members make 10 requests of their leaders:

1. Coordination rather than control
2. Accessibility rather than inaccessibility or omnipresence
3. Information without overload
4. Feedback instead of advice
5. Fairness over favoritism
6. Decisiveness but not intrusive supervision
7. Honesty rather than manipulation
8. Concern for their development over apathy about it
9. Community building over mere coordinated isolation
10. Respect rather than paternalism or condescension

These are not listed in any particular order, with almost all of the expectations being important to employees who have talked to us about distance leadership over the years. Let's review these expectations.

Coordination Rather Than Control

The first expectation is coordination, not control. While team members appreciate attempts at coordination, they normally chafe under what they perceive to be control. Ironically, the best control of the offsite office is the control imposed from within (self-control) rather than from outside (manager-imposed) anyway. So the question is, "How do you encourage self-control without being controlling?" According to Harvard professor Richard Walton, you do it by changing management paradigms from a control orientation to what he calls the commitment paradigm ("From Control to Commitment in the Workplace," *Harvard Business Review*, March–April 1985).

We think he's still right today. Figure 4-1 provides examples of the difference between the control and commitment paradigms.

Control Paradigm	Commitment Paradigm
■ Elicits compliance ■ Believes supervision is necessary ■ Focuses on hierarchy ■ Has a bias for functional organizations ■ Manages by policy ■ Favors audit and enforcement processes ■ Believes in selective information sharing ■ Believes bosses should make decisions ■ Emphasizes means ■ Encourages hard work ■ Rewards conservative improvement ■ Encourages agreement	■ Engenders commitment ■ Believes education is necessary ■ Focuses on customers ■ has a bias for cross-functional organizations ■ Manages by principle ■ Favors learning processes ■ Believes in open information sharing ■ Believes workers should make decisions ■ Emphasizes ends ■ Encourages balanced work/personal life ■ Rewards continuous improvement ■ Encourages thoughtful disagreement

Figure 4-1. Difference between management paradigms

HOW DO YOU BALANCE CONTROL AND COORDINATION? SMART
MANAGING

This is a difficult tightrope to walk. Having too many policies, for example, is often perceived as unnecessary control, while having too few is seen as poor coordination. The key to proper balance is to stay well connected to team members. If you hear things like "We really feel like our hands are tied" or "You haven't given us much choice here," you have probably erred on the side of too much control. Under these conditions, team members generally will not accept ownership or accountability for their work (e.g., "I was just doing what you told me to do" or "That's not my job."). If you hear things like "What are our Paris teammates doing?" or "We're confused because of the inconsistency in how people do things," you have probably erred on the side of not enough coordination. Under these conditions productivity suffers. Being out of balance on either side (control or coordination) affects morale.

Accessibility Rather Than Inaccessibility or Omnipresence

The second expectation is to be accessible. Even if you could be, team members would neither expect nor want you to be physically present all the time. The desire for autonomy in most distance employees is very high. "But" says Mark Nyman, who has worked with numerous virtual teams in several *Fortune* 500 companies, "virtual team members want their leaders to be accessible. They want to know they can reach them when they need to." This doesn't mean virtual team managers need to be on call 24/7, but it usually does mean that they carry cell phones just about everywhere. It also means that they make the extra effort of telling team members when they are not accessible due to vacation, illness, or personal reasons. This extra courtesy creates a sort of virtual leadership presence that employees feel they have some control over.

Information Without Overload

The third expectation is information without overload. If information is the lifeblood of virtual teams, the challenge for the distance manager is to provide people with what they need to sustain their health without unintentionally creating internal hemorrhaging from too much data. Keep them informed but not inundated. Explains Mike Kuczwara, senior human resources manager at Procter & Gamble, "What I want from a virtual team manager is to keep me informed. That's something my manager is really good at. He has the responsibility of managing a human

---

MISTAKE PROOFING

REQUIRED INFORMATION VARIES FROM TEAM TO TEAM

The right balance of information is difficult to maintain, and it may differ significantly from team to team. What is too much information for one team (We can't get anything done because we have too many meetings!) may be too little for another (How do you expect us to get our work done when we don't know what is going on?).

Unfortunately, the technologies to facilitate information passing among team members can also inundate them with unnecessary detail or redundancy. When you do find the right balance, team members are appreciative. For more tips on how to deal with problems such as e-mail glut, see later chapters.

---

resources team where the team members are on the road most of the time. They operate from several locations spread across the country. Something that he does that we all really appreciate is send us a weekly correspondence with key issues and facts in summary form."

Feedback Instead of Advice

The fourth expectation is feedback. People generally appreciate skillfully delivered information about how they are doing. James Gautier is a member of a virtual team of middle school consultants. This team meets together physically only a few times each year. "One thing I really appreciate," says Gautier, "is getting feedback. Sometimes one of the other consultants will sit in on a presentation I'm doing and tell me how they think it was received or Jim (the team leader) will let me know how the teachers and administrators evaluated the session. That helps when you don't have your leader or peers around all the time."

"What most people dislike," clarifies Dee Oviatt, a consulting team member at Pioneer Hi-Bred International, "isn't getting negative feedback about their performance, it's getting inappropriate advice." While appropriate advice is helpful, inappropriate advice (not work related, unsolicited, too superficial, not based on a full understanding of the situation, etc.) can have a dramatic negative effect on morale. While people want mentoring, they don't want meddling. There is a difference. Saying something like, "Miko, I thought it was really helpful to the team when you offered Jacob technical advice in our last Web conference," is mentor-

---

MENTORING VERSUS MEDDLING

How can you tell if you're mentoring or meddling? One way is to wait for the teaching moment when an employee solicits advice. Another is to be careful about how you word things. Saying something like "Paul, your clients let me know they loved your last visit because you took the time to listen to their concerns. They'd like to see that more often" is better than "Paul, you need to listen to your clients."

One is feedback based on data or observation. The other is unsolicited advice. The problem with giving a lot of advice (especially general advice) as a virtual team manager is that the team member often wonders how you would be in a position to offer it when you aren't with them very often.

---

ing. Saying, "Miko, you're too quiet in meetings. Speak up," is meddling. You offered nothing specifically helpful to her (Speak up how? Speak up when?), and only left her concerned that you don't approve of her behavior in meetings. That kind of comment does more harm than good.

Fairness over Favoritism

The next expectation is to be treated fairly. Fairness generally ranks high in surveys about employee expectations of their leaders. This is especially important in virtual situations because perceived inequities are magnified over time and space. Favoritism of any type can affect the productivity of distance workers. "Why should I work so hard," they rationalize, "when results count for less than whether the manager likes you or not?"

In addition to the obvious problems of allowing certain team members to be perceived as favorites (e.g., "He always gets the good assignments" or "Why does she always get the best resources for her projects?"), effective virtual team managers avoid being site-, time-, or culture-centric. It isn't fair, for example, if the same people always have to get out of bed for teleconferences. It isn't fair if people who don't speak English are always left to fend for themselves during meetings. It isn't fair if the same people always travel long distances for the face-to-face meetings. Good virtual team managers assiduously avoid these inequities and are willing to share in the sacrifice required of members of a virtual team. That is part of being the living example mentioned in the previous chapter. If you aren't willing to take your turn getting up at night for a global meeting, or to come in on night shift, or travel to a remote location for a meeting, why should they?

Decisiveness but Not Intrusive Supervision

The sixth expectation is appropriate decisiveness. Team members don't want intrusive supervision, but they don't want you to be among the missing, either. When a leadership decision needs to be made, make it. Although team members want to be involved in decisions that affect the way they do their work, there are certain decisions that you need to make by yourself.

The most obvious example of this is disciplinary action. Few things are more demotivating to a team than when leaders don't resolve employee performance problems. Unresolved incompetence, perpetual lack of safe behaviors, unfulfilled customer requirements, or more blatant individual problems such as dishonesty or sexual harassment can quickly derail a whole team—even at a distance. A good coach (another one of the key competencies noted in the last chapter) knows how to work with people to help them improve. You might receive additional information for your company's specific approach to these problems through your human resources representative.

Although 360-degree feedback activities where peer feedback is received from other team members are becoming common, group disciplinary decisions are still unusual, particularly in virtual teams where the leader may have as much interaction with the team members as their noncollocated peers do. Do not abdicate these types of performance decisions.

Honesty Rather Than Manipulation

Another clear expectation is honesty. In their research on employee expectations of leaders, Kouzes and Posner found that the number-one concern was honesty of leadership (*The Leadership Challenge: How to Get Extraordinary Things Done in Organizations*, Jossey-Bass, 1987). What was true then may even be more true in the current business environment. We have heard similar expectations from numerous team members we have talked with since the global recession of 2008–2010.

They saw overly publicized mismanagement and deception (especially if they were in the financial or insurance sectors) on a scale so large that they couldn't ignore it. It affected their expectations of leaders. They don't want to be manipulated into false participation where the leader tries to get them to agree to his or her way of thinking. They also don't want sugarcoating. They certainly don't want things to be hidden from them.

Concern for Their Development versus Apathy About It

The eighth expectation is that the distance leader will train and develop the team members. This is especially important to employees who feel disconnected from the rest of the organization. Although perceptive employees realize that the days of employment security and company-driven career planning are gone, they do want to know that their leader genuinely cares about their professional development. Employees generally believe that organizations that focus time and energy on employee development are more likely to be successful, viable operations than those that don't. They are also happiest when they believe they are being groomed not only for their current role and responsibilities but for future assignments, as well.

Employees expect that you will be concerned about getting them trained in three categories: (1) business training to better understand their customers, markets, competitors, and financials, (2) technical training to learn how to operate the technologies necessary for them to do their jobs, and (3) interpersonal training to work more effectively with you and their teammates in areas such as effective problem solving, decision making, conflict resolution, and the giving and receiving of feedback. Remember that classroom training isn't always the best way to develop these skills. The most effective learning often occurs from developmental project assignments or mentoring programs.

Community Building versus Mere Coordinated Isolation

The ninth expectation has special importance to remote workers. Virtual team members often experience a feeling of isolation that comes from not working near the rest of their teammates and leaders. The most effective managers help them overcome these concerns through team-building activities and other community-building interventions like those mentioned later in the book. Helping them deal with their feelings of isolation requires more than connecting them electronically with you and their peers—that's only coordinated isolation. Building a team takes more effort. It takes work to clarify the team charter, establish operating guidelines, and get to know the other team members.

This is more important than it appears at first blush. For example, one virtual team member confided to us that although the team she worked on was successful in accomplishing the project on time and within budget, the personal toll was too great. "I would never do it again," she said. "It was too hard to receive feedback on my work from people I didn't know and consequently couldn't respect. My leader didn't handle it well. She only focused on getting the task done. We burned out. Our work could have been better. Just taking the time to help us get to know each other would have made the work go faster and better in the long run. I felt like a robot instead of a human member of a team."

Respect versus Paternalism or Condescension

The final expectation is to be respected. Respect is a basic human need. When it's absent in a society, people revolt. In a business they may become cynical, apathetic, or nonproductive. While they certainly do not want condescending behavior from their leaders, they also do not want the paternalism exhibited by many well-intended corporations. Unfortunately, both condescending behavior and paternalistic behavior send the same unintended message to the recipient: "You can't take care of yourself so I'm going to take care of you." Even in the best of circumstances this approach can create unhealthy dependence, lower self-esteem, and stunt self-initiative.

KEY TERMS

Condescension Speaking to adults like they are children. Saying things like, "You have to check with me before you talk to engineering" leaves the impression that you don't trust your team members or that you think they are dim-witted or irresponsible. Condescension is a cousin to paternalism.

Paternalism Another way to speak to adults like they are children, but it is generally done with the intention of being helpful or protective. Unfortunately, saying something like "I'll take care of speaking to engineering; you don't have to worry about that" can also leave the impression that you don't think the team member is capable of handling an assignment.

Instead of condescending or paternalistic approaches, consider coaching the individuals to learn the skills necessary to do the work themselves.

Manager's Checklist for Chapter 4

☑ Remote employees have 10 common requests for virtual team managers: (1) coordination rather than control, (2) accessibility rather than inaccessibility or omnipresence, (3) information without overload, (4) feedback instead of advice, (5) fairness over favoritism, (6) decisiveness but not intrusive supervision, (7) honesty rather than manipulation, (8) concern for their development over apathy about it, (9) community building over mere coordinated isolation, and (10) respect rather than paternalism or condescension.

☑ The control paradigm is a common type of management thinking. It is based on the idea that the manager's job is to control people. Unfortunately, it usually backfires in a virtual team situation.

☑ The commitment paradigm is a different way of thinking about management. It assumes that the job of the manager is not to control people, but to create an environment in which they can control themselves.

☑ Controlling processes instead of people enables the virtual team manager to empower people. It's an approach more consistent with the commitment paradigm than the control paradigm, and it helps the leader ensure that employees are productive whether or not the leader is present.

Note

An earlier version of this chapter was published in *The Distance Manager* (McGraw-Hill, 2001), and this version of the chapter is used by permission of the authors and copyright holders.

Bridging Cultural Differences

The way a team plays as a whole determines its success. You may
have the greatest bunch of individual stars in the world, but if they
don't play together, the club won't be worth a dime.

—Babe Ruth

A we have already mentioned, one of the great challenges of virtual
teams is that they typically offer great cultural diversity. Leverag-
ing the advantages and managing the challenges of diverse cultural backgrounds is vital to the development and strength of any virtual
team. To introduce this topic, let's consider a case study about a hypo-
thetical company called TechWorld. This case is based on slightly modified challenges faced by a number of our clients.

TechWorld Mini-Case Study

Ahmed Araz is the team leader for a group of 12 design engineers in
TechWorld, a large transnational company. He was promoted to team
leader a year ago just a few months after TechWorld acquired another
high-tech firm, Micro Works. Ahmed and three of the other engineers are
located in Palo Alto, California, three are in Seattle, two are in Tokyo,
three in Dublin, and one in Munich. The engineers in Seattle and Dublin
were part of Micro Works.

The team was formed three months ago and has been chartered to develop the next generation of TechWorld's Voice over Internet Protocol (VoIP) product. So far, Ahmed feels things are going fairly well, although a few issues have caught his attention. Last week Gavin and Michelle in the Seattle office called Ahmed to complain that Johan from the Munich office wasn't keeping the commitments he made at the last teleconference and so the project was already three weeks behind schedule. They complained that when they called him, he seemed offended at their inquiry and told them he reported to Ahmed, not them. They said they were especially frustrated because when a similar incident occurred with the Palo Alto engineers, they confronted them and talked it out in a 30-minute teleconference, and things were back on schedule within two days. "If Johan can't be a team player," they moaned, "how can we ever get this project completed on time?"

Adam, Sam, and Fiona, who make up the Palo Alto contingent, seem to work well with the rest of the team, although they do occasionally throw in a comment or two about TechNext, an initiative introduced two years ago that defines a clear process for getting products designed and onto the market in record time. TechNext was introduced with a great deal of fanfare and was seen by TechWorld as the answer to rapid design and development. Ahmed hasn't heard any direct feedback about how the team members from Micro Works feel about TechNext, but he has noticed an underlying tension when the Palo Alto members tout it as "the way we do things at TechWorld." Most of the Dublin and Seattle groups seem reluctant to embrace some of the concepts, and when the team set up its project plan, they argued for a less aggressive schedule.

Ahmed is also a bit worried because Miyoki and Keiko from the Tokyo office seem reticent to jump in during teleconferences. Their work is impeccable, but they just aren't talking during team discussions. He really wants their input, because in terms of technical knowledge, they are probably the strongest members of the team.

Although John, Matthew, and Ryan in the Dublin plant drag their feet a little, they are great guys. They don't seem to have any issues, other than they like to make a lot of comments during team meetings on the U.S. political system and its export/import laws. So far the comments haven't caused much stir—in fact, a couple of the U.S. engineers have said they agreed. But Ahmed worries that at some point someone will get offended and progress on the project will suffer.

When Ahmed took this assignment, he worried about trying to coordinate the project from so many locations. But he thought that, given the professional level and skill of the team members, they could do most of the problem resolution without him needing to intervene. "How concerned should I be about these issues?" he wonders.

Case Review

A review of this case surfaces many of the challenges associated with managing cultural differences. For example, although the case concerns a global team, there are more cultural issues here than the ones presented by the U.S., Japanese, Irish, and German geographic cultures. One of these problems is the misalignment of the TechWorld and Micro Works organizational cultures. This is especially problematic because most of the former Micro Works employees refuse to use the TechWorld product development and introduction process, causing potential delays in the project schedule.

Stereotypes versus Generalizations. Because most of us recognize the negative consequences of stereotyping, a legitimate concern often raised when addressing the topic of culture is that such a discussion may leave the group divided or individuals mistreated. In their book *Doing Business Internationally*, Walker, Walker, and Schmitz (McGraw Hill, 2003) make a clear distinction between stereotyping and what they call "generalization." One fosters cultural understanding, whereas the other discourages it.

To effectively address the challenges of cultural differences, it's important to have a point from which to launch a discussion. That is where generalizations like "Many Germans see realistic deadlines as fixed and inflexible targets rather than as a business variable to be negotiated" may be helpful to begin a conversation. But generalizations provide a constructive framework only if we keep in mind that they are a starting point from which a rich, open-minded discussion can begin—not the conclusion of the discussion. If they devolve into stereotyping that suggests, for example, that all members of a particular culture always act in a certain way ("Germans are inflexible about time frames"), discussions lock down and often become nonproductive. The real solutions to problems may go unconsidered. People are more complex than stereotypes imply.

If Ahmed in the TechWorld case study, for instance, were to assume that all Germans view deadlines inflexibly, he would probably deal with Johan inappropriately—since Johan's schedule slips suggest he doesn't think that way. Additionally, if Ahmed thought that everyone in the Micro Works culture was resistant to the new product development process, he might offend those who weren't, and not deal effectively with those individuals who were actually causing the delays. And if he assumed that Miyoki and Keiko were hesitant to participate in team meetings because of their Japanese background, he might simply be wrong.

CULTURAL STEREOTYPING

Although generalizations about a culture open the opportunity to discuss legitimate differences among people, stereotyping promotes closed thinking, biased behavior, and bigotry. Always avoid stereotyping.

In the real situation on which this part of the case was based, the Japanese reticence to participate in meetings was caused by a lack of facility in English, not a cultural tendency to avoid participating in meetings. Once the company provided English as second language courses (with special emphasis on technical vocabulary), the reluctance melted away.

How Do Cultures Differ?

Following are some areas in which different cultures typically have different perspectives. Although theses differences may be most obvious with geographic cultures, other types of cultures have them, as well. Unless these are discussed and resolved, some of these issues may reduce the productivity of your virtual team.

For example, a virtual team leader who isn't careful to address cultural differences on the team appropriately will almost certainly have problems with project schedules (as some members of the team assume that a schedule slip is a serious problem, while others don't see it as a big deal), vacation and holiday scheduling (if some team members become offended when they are unable to take time off for their religious celebrations or regional holidays), general interaction and work coverage challenges (as some team members request not to work on certain assignments with individuals of a particular gender, race, religion, or ethnicity), or morale (when some team members are offended when others make insensitive comments, use certain gestures, or eat certain foods in their presence). Almost all these types of problems can be lessened, if not avoided entirely, through sensitive education and communication. Here are some more areas to consider.

Time

How does each team member view time? Are deadlines set in stone, or are they a guideline or starting point for further discussion as a task or project progresses? Should meetings start promptly, or is it acceptable to be a few minutes late? And once the team is all assembled, is it best to launch right into the agenda, or is it more appropriate or polite to first mingle socially for a period of time?

PROMPT—OR NOT

FOR EXAMPLE

One of the team managers we worked with was frustrated when part of his new virtual team, which was located on a South Seas island, was late on a key project deadline. These team members also were late to the first project team web conference, delaying the meeting start for about 20 minutes. At first the manager was concerned that he had a performance problem to work with, and he steeled himself to take the first step in the company progressive disciplinary process. But when he spoke to the islanders about the problem, they were upset and apologetic. Their previous work experiences with local companies had put a low priority on promptness and higher priorities on a warm and friendly atmosphere. When they understood the new expectation, they modified their behavior to the norm of the U.S.-based company, but would have been unlikely to do so had the manager not brought the cultural difference to their attention.

Relationships

Relationships are integral to a team's success. It's important, therefore, to understand differences in how teammates approach the development and maintenance of relationships. For instance, how quickly do they trust other teammates? Do they assume all are trustworthy until proven otherwise, or does their cultural experience suggest that trust is earned over time? Is engaging in team-building activities a good way to build rapport on the team, or is that a waste of time? How should conflicts be handled? Do they prefer to address them head on and get things out in the open, or is that approach seen as overly aggressive or unprofessional?

Later in the book we discuss a tool called operating guidelines that help in situations like this to create positive relationships. And in the chapter on creating trust, we offer several suggestions on how to create a trusting team culture, regardless of the national cultures of the team members.

Communication

At least two aspects of communication need to be considered relative to culture—technology use and style. Technology-use protocols are discussed in detail later in the book as a way to bridge differences about technology use. The style component of communication is a bit trickier to manage.

> **KEY TERM**
>
> **Communication style** The tone or feel of verbal or written interactions between people. Each person has a unique communication style that is influenced by a number of cultural factors including his or her upbringing and education. One's communication style is more than the selection of words, phrases, and intonation. It includes, for example, what one chooses to speak about or not speak about, when one chooses to intervene or remain quiet, and how formal or deferential one is.

In some cultures (geographic, organizational, or life style, for example) it's rude to address conflict or give feedback directly, while in other cultures not doing so is seen as evasive or weak. In some cultures, an informal approach to communication is the norm, including the use of slang terms and calling co-workers and bosses by first names or nicknames. In other cultures, however, such informality is seen as unprofessional or disrespectful.

Cultural biases can also dictate credibility when communicating. For instance, one culture may defer to those with the most technical knowledge; others may let titles or positions determine who gets listened to; in still other cultures, status is determined by any number of factors such as age, gender, discipline, education, seniority, government, or military experience. A virtual team may have difficulty making a decision, for example, if a respected member isn't present or doesn't agree. Or the team members may defer to certain individuals even if that deference is non-functional. A knowledgeable team leader can make a huge difference in team effectiveness by understanding this dynamic. Assigning a particular person to a project, for example, can sometimes guarantee either success or failure, not because of the team member's personal expertise or competence, but only because of how these cultural factors affect the person and his or her relationship to the team.

A team leader we know worked with one team, for example, where people from Vietnam and Cambodia were in the majority. Multiple requests from corporate headquarters to encourage the team to make some procedural changes went unanswered until the team leader discovered that the informal leader of the team, a former senior officer in the Vietnamese army, had not been consulted about the matter. Even though this man was technically a peer to the other team members, once the manager discussed the problem with the respected peer and got his agreement to the change, the respected peer convinced the others to make the procedural modifications in only a few days. Had the manager neglected this step, the change would likely never have happened.

Boss/Subordinate Roles

Perception of how the manager is supposed to operate or what the management role is varies widely across cultures. In some, if the manager attempts to be democratic or participative, he or she is seen as effective. In others, the opposite happens. Some cultures expect the manager to solicit employee feedback, while others view that as weakness or ineptitude.

Space

Is the corner office with the view a coveted spot, or is there greater honor in sitting in the midst of the team? Are people who work from their home disadvantaged because the home office is less prestigious than ones in an office building?

How personal space is viewed is important. In some cultures getting physically close to someone when talking is seen as a sign of respect or trust, while in other cultures it makes people uncomfortable and is con-

CLARIFY YOUR STYLE

Due to differing cultural norms around management, it's important that you explicitly clarify how you view your role and how you want to work with people. If you don't, the existing cultural preferences will prevail. Some people on the team may view your behavior as too weak, while others see the same behavior as overbearing due to their cultural biases about how managers should act in a particular circumstance.

If, for example, you intend to be a participative manager and you know that certain members of your team will, due to their cultural backgrounds, see that as weak management, you might say something like, "I have become convinced that good management requires getting ideas from my team. I know that some of you think that managers should make all the decisions without employee involvement, but I'm not going to work that way. I think we'll get better results by working together."

sidered an infringement on their personal space. You may not even see this until at your first face-to-face meeting, some employees report that other people are "acting weird" or "making them feel uncomfortable."

Use of the Body

The use of the human body along with common physical gestures differs from culture to culture. When referring to themselves, for example, some people point to one part of the body whereas others point to another part. Some express greetings in one way, whereas others use a different way. The gesture in one culture for "come here" might actually mean "go away" in another. In some cultures it's okay to touch another person, but in others it is strictly forbidden. Looking someone in the eye shows courtesy in some cultures and disrespect in others. Common gestures in one culture may be seen as rude or even offensive in others.

Although these issues may seem insignificant, they might be the reason why confusion ensues after a Web conference ("Hey, I thought you *didn't* want me to help you" or "I thought you were talking about somebody else, *not yourself*"). Worse, they may cause unintended offense that gets in the way of collaboration ("I'm not working with that man. He hates me. Why else would he have shown me the bottom of his feet"). New virtual managers are often surprised at how passionate and disruptive these concerns can be.

CULTURE CONFLICT

SMART

MANAGING

Some cultural team dynamics that are potentially problematic and require change may only surface in face-to-face meetings. When team members, for example, avoid members of their team at a face-to-face meeting because they "smell bad" (different diet or hygiene habits), or "act weird" (sit too close to them, sit too far away, look them in the eyes, don't look them in the eyes, won't talk to them because they are women, talk to them in spite of the fact that they are married women, etc.), the team leader has to make a determination whether to address the issue or not.

Sometimes it's not worth it to intervene, because the cultural dynamics that show up in face-to-face meetings may have little effect on the normal working relationships of team members who mostly connect with each other virtually. But if these dynamics are symptoms of a bigger problem, and indicate that a lack of understanding or sensitivity about other cultures might be getting in the way of people working with each other virtually, they need to be addressed.

How can you make a judgment about this when you have so little first-hand experience? Ask yourself if the way people act together face-to-face is an indication of a virtual work problem. For example, does the fact that Joseph and Mira didn't talk together in the meeting make you wonder if their lack of coordination in the project teleconference last week was more than a mutual bad day as you originally assumed? Team members don't have to be friends. They don't even have to like each other. But if culturally related prejudices make people unwilling to work together, or insensitivity to other cultures causes hurt feelings that impede communication and collaboration, you have to intervene.

The solution may be something easy such as doing team-building exercises or creating an excuse for team members to get to know each other better as human beings. Try having everyone spend a few minutes talking about his or her family. It's often something as simple as that that breaks the ice in a virtual team relationship and helps establish the trust that fosters improved interactions.

Or it may take something more, such as cross-cultural sensitivity training or conflict resolution training. In rare cases the problem can be even more serious. If you discover that deep-seated or irreversible cultural biases exist on your team (members of warring ethnic groups or religious sects, for example), you may have to adjust your staffing.

Dealing with Different Country-of-Origin Cultures

A number of resources can help you identify and discuss differing country-of-origin culture issues on your team (e.g., kissbowshakehands.com).

Cultural sensitivity awareness training can also help teams address these issues. Teaching language classes may be helpful in this regard. The virtual team leaders we work with often recommend that, at a minimum, the manager learn key words and phrases in the major language groups used on his or her team. Unless you become fluent, this may not improve communication, but it often shows team members you care enough about them to make an effort.

In our experience, however, it's nearly impossible for you or the other team members to ever become fully aware of all the potential tripwires associated with geographic cultures. There are several problems:

Any attempt to reduce a significant country culture to a written description is bound to contain errors and oversights. In one discussion we had with a client, for example, we referred to an authoritative resource that described the cultural differences between North and South India. After reading the work together, we asked if it was accurate.

Several of the Indians in the room agreed that the book had some useful generalizations about their geographic and religious cultures, but they complained that the write-up didn't recognize the far bigger differences between the cultures of rural versus urban India or highly educated versus less-educated people. Plus, as we've mentioned before, it's ridiculous to assume that even the majority of a particular culture will consistently think or act in a predictable way. Thinking that these resources will make you an expert may lead you to say things that make you appear foolish or inexperienced in front of your team. Losing your team's respect will only make your job more difficult.

Many people in organizations today have had life experiences in many geographic cultures. In one workshop we taught recently, 90 percent of the people had lived in three or more countries and spoke at least two languages. When we asked people to identify the primary geographic or country-of-origin culture that influenced their thinking or behavior, more than three-quarters said, "a mixture."

This is also common in younger generations that often identify culturally with people their own age across multiple countries (perhaps as a function of global TV, movie, music, and Internet access) even more than with their own genetic heritage. One of the authors speaks Japanese as a second language and lived for two years in Japan. During that time, the older generation referred to the younger generation by the *Japanese* word "new homosapien." When he told his Japanese colleagues that term was an English one that meant different species of human, they were sometimes surprised, but nearly always agreed it was appropriate.

People tend to be a composite of their life experiences, influenced by a number of things at once: places where they grew up, places they lived, their families, their friends and mentors, their schooling, religion, ethnicity, gender, and above all, their ability as human beings to pick and choose how they will respond in any particular circumstance. It's unusual for the country-of-origin culture to affect an individual to the exclusion of other cultural influences.

That said, it's probably best to be sensitive to the country-of-origin cultures of others without pretending to be an expert on them. What's really important is for you to care about what your team members themselves say about their complex cultural differences and similarities, not to make judgments based on something you read about their country of birth or current location. We recommend that you mostly work on understanding your own cultural biases first, and then be open to discussions about how culture has affected others on your team. If you build an effective team, act like a sensitive and caring person, apologize when you err, and create a team culture of trust, you will likely be forgiven most of your cultural trespasses.

CULTURAL BLINDNESS

We can't help but see other cultures through the lens of our own experience. That's why we sometimes think eating some food, making some gesture, or responding in a particular way is "weird." We're judging another's behavior against our standard, not against that person's cultural standard (in which that person's behavior makes perfect sense). To be sensitive to the cultures of others, it helps to understand the cultures that have influenced our own thinking and behavior. This allows us to see that our way is only one of the many ways in which the world can make sense to someone. Even if we don't become experts in all cultures, we will learn to be sensitive to the cultural views of others.

WHO ARE YOU?

FOR EXAMPLE The way people answer the questions "Who are you?" or "What do you do?" is an interesting way to elicit cultural differences. When we ask these questions in the United States, for example, we normally hear people answer with a title or function such as "I'm a vice president" or "I'm an attorney." But in the Mideast, Africa, or Slavic countries we are more likely to hear family roles, religious affiliation, or ethnicity, such as "I'm a father of three sons" or "I am Shia" or "I am Zulu."

Cultural Self-Awareness Assessment

To learn more about your own cultural biases, answer the following cultural awareness questions. Then pair up with someone who you believe has a cultural background different from your own. Compare and contrast your answers. This might be an interesting discussion to have with your team.

Cultural Awareness Assessment

1. Who are you? How do you describe who you are?
2. What are the cultures that make you who you are?
3. How do you view deadlines? Are they generally fixed or flexible?
4. How do you view time relative to meetings (e.g., start/stop times, breaks, adherence to an agenda, etc.)?
5. How important is it to you to be prompt? How important is it to you that others are prompt?
6. How do you feel about socializing with co-workers?
7. What is the best way to deal with conflict?
8. What is the best way to solve problems?
9. What is the best way to make decisions?
10. What is the best way to communicate with co-workers?
11. What is the role of the manager?
12. How do you feel about your manager asking for input or increasing employee involvement in your team?
13. What is the role of employees who are not managers?
14. How should acceptable behavior or accomplishments be rewarded?
15. How should unacceptable behavior be addressed?

16. Give three examples of rude or inappropriate behavior.
17. What constitutes success for your team?
18. What would constitute a failure?
19. How is space viewed in your location?
20. How do you view your personal space?

TOOLS FOR BRIDGING CULTURE GAPS

TOOLS

Teams need diversity. It naturally enriches their thinking, instills greater creativity, and provides a cross-section of skills. But how does the team overcome the myriad of challenges that cultural differences may introduce and still perform at exceptional levels?

Being culturally aware of others is the first step, but most teams find that they need to create a culture of their own that allows all members to bridge the diversity gap and focus on the same things. Three tools that facilitate the creation of a powerful homogenous virtual team culture (even in a very diverse team) are:

- A clear charter
- Operating guidelines
- Technology-use protocols

These tools are discussed in detail later in the book.

Culture may be the most difficult of the three key variables (space, time, and culture) to manage. But when done well, it has a powerful motivating and aligning effect on virtual team members. When a manager isn't around to instruct, train, or inspire a virtual team member, the team member will most likely take direction from the cultural "script" that most influences him or her. Therefore, most teams find it essential to create a productive team culture that will supersede the potentially misaligning effects of multiple individual cultures. We show you how to do that in later chapters.

Manager's Checklist for Chapter 5

☑ Helping virtual teams create their own unique culture may be the most pragmatic way to deal with the inevitable distractions that can be caused by a variety of separate cultures on the team. Later in the book we discuss tools, such as operating guidelines, for doing this.

☑ One of the most important things you can do is learn to be sensitive to the culture of others. You will never have the time to become a cultural expert in every culture you will encounter.

☑ One reason it's difficult to become a credible expert in other geographic cultures is that simple descriptions of a culture that covers a vast area (such as a country) are bound to contain errors or omissions. Another reason is that we live in a mobile, global society in which many people have life experiences in a variety of geographic cultures. So, for example, even if you were an expert in both countries in which one of your team members lived, you would have no way to know what parts of what culture applied to that person. And third, people can choose to accept or reject cultural influences. We are all individuals, influenced, but not enslaved, by our upbringing.

☑ Some things our cultural upbringings are likely to influence include our perspectives on time, relationships (including preferences about trust building and conflict resolution), communication (both technology use and style), boss/subordinate roles, space, and use of the body (especially the use of gestures). Each of these perspectives affects collaboration and can be a potential area of conflict that requires management intervention to resolve.

☑ A great place to start to become culturally sensitive is to really think about your own culture(s). What life experiences have made you who you are? Since we always see other's cultures through the lens of our own, it is important to be aware of what our glasses look like.

☑ Although it's important to be aware of cultural differences, it is dangerous to engage in cultural stereotyping.

☑ There are many types of cultures, including geographic, socioeconomic, racial, religious, gender, educational, organizational, and life style. Assuming that any person is affected by only one type of culture is naive.

Note

Much of this information is excerpted from a workbook entitled *Bridging Cultural Distances* (The Fisher Group, Inc., 2010) that we use to train clients. Used by permission of the authors and copyright holders.

Chapter 6

Starting Up (or Refocusing) a Virtual Team

Coming together is a beginning. Keeping together is progress. Working together is success.

—Henry Ford

I n several of the preceding chapters we referred to a number of tools that help virtual teams create a functional culture and address many of the problems common to virtual teams. In this chapter we discuss those tools. They include charters, role clarification, and operating guidelines, and we show you how you can employ these three tools to make your virtual teams more effective.

Virtual teams often report that their members suffer from a series of challenges, including using collaboration technologies effectively, overcoming feelings of isolation, and misalignments around tasks, purpose, and operating procedures. To deal with these challenges as efficiently and effectively as possible, most virtual teams find that some sort of face-to-face start-up activity that includes purposing and culture development is essential. Even if the team has been together for years, we recommend a face-to-face meeting periodically to align and refocus the team. Although the tools we explain here are ideal for use when starting up a team, they also work well for refocusing existing teams.

Many managers are not able to select the members of their team. But if you are in the enviable position of being able to start up a virtual team from scratch, or even lucky enough to participate in the selection of some of your virtual team, there are some things you should consider.

Selecting Virtual Team Members

The effectiveness of a virtual team depends heavily on its membership. Working virtually can be both exciting and challenging. Some individuals, for instance, may enjoy the opportunity to work with others from a variety of cultures and geographic locations, but find the isolation associated with working from a distance to be difficult. Therefore, thoughtful selection and careful orientation of new team members are crucial to ensure that the new members understand and are prepared for what working virtually entails.

There are several characteristics to look for when selecting individuals to work on virtual teams. In addition to education and prior work background, the following are attributes or skills to consider when selecting virtual workers. Each team needs to carefully evaluate which of these are most critical for its situation.

- Works independently with minimal supervision
- Enjoys working on a team
- Is a self-starter
- Demonstrates self-discipline
- Gets good results
- Demonstrates competence with both work and communication technologies
- Demonstrates good judgment
- Demonstrates good interpersonal skills (such as collaborating effectively, listening, giving and receiving feedback, resolving conflict, etc.)
- Demonstrates willingness to take accountability

Let's review these skills and attributes in more detail.

Individuals who enjoy working alone, but are not antisocial loners. Those who tend to do best on virtual teams are those who like working alone, but who aren't antisocial loners. Placing a self-professed "loner" in a remote situation could prove to be problematic. The isolation could exacerbate the problems resulting from what may already be a self-imposed lack of contact with others, thus rendering him or her ineffective in making decisions, solving problems, or seizing opportunities for personal growth. Look for individuals who can complete assignments on time while working alone, but who actively seek out others to share ideas, gain input, and socialize.

Self-starters who exhibit strong self-discipline. Individuals working in virtual settings need to be self-starters who require little prodding to keep projects or other work moving forward. Virtual team members must understand that working from a distance doesn't mean a break in the action or a chance to fool around. As one wise manager of virtual teams noted, "The system will fail if the team is made up of the type of people who need constant prodding to get the work done."

Technological competence. Working virtually depends heavily on the use of current technologies for communication, problem solving, project planning, etc. Therefore, proficiency with computers, e-mail, intranets, social networking, various Web tools, etc., is essential. Keep in mind that if people in remote locations don't already have these basic skills, it may be difficult to train them in your specific applications.

Good judgment. Working across distance and time almost guarantees that individuals will be required to make critical decisions on their own. Thus, an ability to employ good judgment in a timely way is crucial.

Good interpersonal skills. An inability to work well with others becomes magnified across distance. Poor interpersonal skills often result in the individual being ineffective in his or her contribution as other team members quickly discover how easy it is to "lock" someone out when that person isn't physically present. If the team is unable to access information and knowledge from an individual, it can jeopardize both the success of a given project and the future of the team member.

Willingness to take accountability for results—both personal and business. The effectiveness of a dispersed team depends in large measure on each individual's willingness to find ways to help the team be successful. Initiating ways to share learnings with remote colleagues, rather than lamenting the fact that they aren't in the next cubicle, might be one example of this willingness to assume accountability. Individuals eager to make a less-than-perfect situation work are more likely to succeed in a virtual setting than those prone to feeling like "victims" when things don't go their way.

Other tools, such as personality profiling, can provide insight into one's aptitude for working alone. These can be helpful when used in conjunction with tools such as adequate skills training. But most important is that the virtual team manager and the team be as frank as possible during the hiring process about the isolation that is common in these types of teams. Ask applicants for examples of when they have successfully operated this way before, and listen carefully to the way they talk about it. Do they sound happy? Sad? Frustrated? A rule of thumb in the behavioral sciences field is that past behavior is the best predictor of future behavior. If an individual liked working remotely before and was successful, she or he will probably enjoy it and be successful again. If the individual didn't enjoy it, or struggled to be productive, it probably isn't a good match.

ASK FOR EXAMPLES
Don't ask candidates if they are self-starters or have a particular skill set or attitude. Of course they'll say what they think you want to hear. Instead, ask them for examples of when they displayed that attribute. Dig into the details with follow-up questions until you and your team really understand a person's experience, results, and work preferences. And remember to talk to your human resources professional before you start a selection process. Be very clear on what kind of questions you can and cannot ask. If you or your team say the wrong thing, you may be exposing your company to a lawsuit.

When interviewing candidates for a virtual team, whether the assignment is for a project that will only last for a few months or for a long-term placement that may last several years, you should probably ask a lot of questions. Professional interviewers normally plan to speak only about 10 percent of the time, using 90 percent of the time to listen to the candidate. That requires both a skill in asking open-ended questions (to generate something more than yes or no answers) and the patience to listen carefully.

EXAMPLES OF QUESTIONS TO ASK POTENTIAL VIRTUAL TEAM MEMBERS

- Give me an example of a time when you had to do something without supervision. Specifically, what was the situation?
- How did it work out? What results occurred?
- What did you like and dislike most about that situation?
- In the absence of supervision, how did you keep yourself motivated?
- What did you do to stay organized?
- How did you interact with other members of your team?
- What worked and what didn't work so well?
- Did you learn anything from this experience that made you do something different later?
- How did that second situation turn out?

Orientation for New Virtual Team Members

In addition to careful selection, a comprehensive orientation process that explains the organization's culture, introduces other teammates, and clarifies the roles and responsibilities of all team members helps ensure a smooth transition and long-term success. Consider the following suggestions and whether they could be of use in your virtual team:

Provide training that paints a realistic picture of what it will be like working remotely. It may be helpful, for instance, to invite people who have worked on virtual teams to provide their perspectives, both positive and negative. A panel discussion, for example, with time allotted for questions and answers, can be very effective. Visits to satellite sites also provide a first-hand look at how the distance office is set up and how the accompanying technology is used to make the virtual situation workable. If the person will be working at home, have him or her talk to others about managing a home office and dealing with the inevitable distractions of that environment.

Take time to conduct an in-depth introduction of the new employee to other team members. Have him or her spend phone or online time with fellow team members to understand what each member's role is and how it integrates with the rest of the team.

Include a thorough discussion of the organization's culture. Provide historical information and describe any organizational nuances or idiosyncrasies

 **INCLUDE THE TEAM!** Including the team in the selection and orientation processes ensures that a new team member will get a better start. It also makes it more likely that (1) you'll get the best candidate for the position and, even more importantly, that (2) the team will help the new member be successful afterward. The members of the team are more likely to work with somebody they selected than somebody you selected for them.

that might be useful to know when working across departments or functions. If possible, create the opportunity for the new team member to have frank discussions with others about organizational politics and other realities they must deal with to be effective.

Review the team's charter and operating guidelines. Provide background on each of these tools (we review in detail later in this chapter), and then get verbal agreement from the new team member to support them. It's also a good idea to give him or her an opportunity to offer suggestions or additions to these two documents.

Review the team's communication protocols and preferences. Be sure to capture the new team member's preferences and share them with the rest of the team.

Set aside sufficient time for the new employee to get up to speed on the technologies the team uses. This may include a variety of communication technologies.

If this is a project team, provide current status and history of the project. Include a discussion of why the project was established and the timelines crucial to the team's success.

Build in some face-to-face time with the team as soon as possible. This is a good idea for a team to do periodically, but is especially critical when a new member is brought on board. Until people meet face-to-face, it's more difficult to have a trusting culture.

Creating a Team Charter

A good place to start creating a functional virtual team culture is with a chartering activity. A team charter is a statement of joint purpose created by and agreed to by all team members. The charter discussion allows each team member to express his or her views on what the team's core purpose and objectives are, thus clarifying early on where time and energy will be focused and how relative priorities will be determined.

> **Charter** A brief statement that clarifies the purpose of the team. It normally includes things like key deliverables, deadlines, customers, and priorities.
>
> **KEY TERM**

Team members often have their own ideas of what the team is supposed to do, and those ideas are often not aligned because team members don't have much opportunity to rub shoulders with one another in a series of work activities that may create a common focus. For example, one virtual product development team struggled because many of the engineers had different ideas about the team's purpose. Some people thought their purpose was to produce leading-edge products others thought they needed to meet customer expectations even if it did not require leading-edge technologies. Still other team members felt that the purpose of the team was to create products that could be easily manufactured and serviced. Such differences of opinion caused confusion and

---

SAMPLE TEAM CHARTER

FOR EXAMPLE

Team Purpose: The purpose of the Accounting Software Implementation Team is to plan and oversee the implementation of the new Enterprise Resource Planning software at company headquarters (Detroit) and each of the company's ten locations (Amsterdam, London, Guadalajara, Sacramento, Omaha, Albany, Houston, Redmond, Tokyo, Hong Kong).

Key Customers: Our primary customers are the company accountants at each site and outside customers and vendors whose money will be processed using the new software.

Key Results: The key results expected from the Accounting Software Implementation Team are:

- Have the program installed and fully operational at all locations by June 30 of next year.
- Keep all payables and receivables personnel fully informed and up to date on the software implementation.
- Ensure all government regulations are met at each site.
- Submit a complete project proposal and timeline within four months.

inefficiencies until they were resolved several months later. If team purpose is not clarified at the onset, team performance will be suboptimal.

The written team charter document is less important than the discussion it represents, and what may seem simplistic or trivial to an outsider may reflect a significant insight or carefully worded resolution of conflicting views to people who participated in the process. It is useful to develop a format for these charters that represents the unique requirements of a particular team, but it is not unusual to include something like an overall purpose statement, clarification of customer requirements, and an inclusion of key deliverables.

The charter need not be long. A more common mistake than too much brevity is a document that is too long to be remembered by its creators. If people cannot remember it, they probably will not use it. The best statements, for example, clearly describe the desired customer experience, and therefore, keep the team focused on adding value from the perspective of the person who pays for the product or service the team members provide.

CHARTERING VIRTUAL TEAMS

FOR EXAMPLE A group of Microsoft executives discovered that a key to solving some of their problems with virtual teams was effective chartering. Notorious for their culture of encouraging very bright people to aggressively build business opportunities, it was not unusual for team members to unintentionally expand their roles into areas for which other teams already had responsibility. To eliminate redundant activity and focus the teams more effectively in areas where untapped opportunity existed, they used chartering tools and realized "significant" business improvements within a matter of only a few weeks.

Practical Tips for Chartering

Make sure you involve key people outside the team as you develop the charter. These people might include customers, managers, or staff and technical support people. In many cases, some of these people will need to provide approval. It's a good idea to involve them early in the process. Project teams, for example, need clarity from the beginning regarding their assignment and the outcomes their leadership expects. A common problem many virtual team members face is *multiplexing*. "Multiplexing" is the pervasive practice of having multiple concurrent assignments. Because they often serve on several different teams simultaneously, it's difficult for virtual team members to plan their time appropriately unless they know the relative priorities of the projects competing for their attention. This issue can be addressed in chartering if the right people are present.

Agree on a tight timeline for completing the chartering process. This is especially important if you cannot meet face-to-face and are creating the charter from a distance using technology. Establishing clear timelines for when team members need to respond to each step of the process is critical. If creating the charter face-to-face, don't let the process drag on. Getting bogged down here can drain energy and result in discouragement. Get the charter to a point that everyone can live with and then revise it later, if necessary.

Strive for practicality, not perfection. No charter is perfect. Don't expect it to describe everything about your team perfectly. Work to make a practical statement that guides the team and provides clarity about what is expected. Keep in mind that the charter can always be revised.

Live by your charter. Creating a charter needs to be more than just an exercise. The result should be a useful tool for keeping the team focused and on track. For this reason, it is a good idea to ask each team member to state his or her commitment to following it. Absent a face-to-face or video venue, a teleconference where each person vocally affirms the charter can suffice.

Role Clarification

The second activity recommended for the virtual team start-up (or refocusing) is the use of a role clarification tool. Because much has been written about these kinds of tools, this chapter does not elaborate, other than to say it is important for virtual team members to have a visual indicator that helps them understand the distinct assignments and responsibilities of each team member. Already handicapped by their lack of easy access to their peers, virtual team members are less likely to collaborate with people with whom they have unclear responsibilities than with those with whom they have clear, shared responsibilities. Many teams we have worked with use something like the RACI or RASCI diagram (Responsible, Approval, Support, Consult, or Inform) and post it on their team Web site. See Figure 6-1 for an example from a wonderful not-for-profit middle school consulting firm we worked with. These types of common project management tools list each person on the team with corresponding information about his or her role on particular project parameters. The team's Web site is also a good place to post a shared calendar that has key project mileposts, operating guidelines, and technology protocols discussed in this chapter.

Decisions	Roles	Lead Team	Site Team	Regional Director	Site Manager	School Consultant	Partnership Manager	Senior Consultant	Team Leader	Tech Team	Tech Team Consultant	All Individuals	Executive Director	Vice President
Calendar		R												
School Expenditures						R								
Tech Team Expenditures									R					
Consultant Travel Expenses												R		
Personnel														R	A
Consultant Contracts													R	A
Partnership Budget													R	A
Operational Policies														
Summer Institute		R												
Regional Conferences			R		S									
Teacher Institute		R												
Site Assignments													C	R
Site Team Budget														

Only one "R" on each horizontal decision line.

R – **Responsibility:** The responsibility to initiate action to ensure the decision is carried out
A – **Approval:** Approval required of the decider. The item must be reviewed by the particular role occupant, and this person has the option of either vetoing or approving.
S – **Support:** Provide logistical support.
C – **Consult:** Get input from but not the right to veto.
I – **Inform:** Be informed, by inference, must not influence.

Figure 6-1. A RASCI role clarification form

> ## CLARIFYING ROLES AND RESPONSIBILITIES
> We have had success in our own firm with a simple but powerful process to clarify roles and responsibilities. At the beginning of each fiscal year, we have a face-to-face strategic planning meeting. Once we have finalized the annual plan, we post a chart pad page on the wall for each of the team members. We each then write on our own chart pad page what we believe we are responsible for this coming year. When each of us has finished our list, we rotate around to each page, and everyone writes down any omissions or disagreements on every other person's list. We conclude the activity by discussing and finalizing each list. It provides a good start to the year and helps everyone feel included in doling out the annual project assignments and reevaluating the other nonproject responsibilities to ensure fairness, growth opportunities, and coverage. Although these lists always have to be modified throughout the year as new projects emerge, the business changes, or assignments get cancelled, the annual discussion provides a good foundation for the modifications.
>
> **TOOLS**

Operating Guidelines

The third focusing tool is operating guidelines, which identify acceptable and unacceptable team behavior. For virtual teams, these become a statement of the shared culture that supersedes the differing functional, geographic, or other subcultures that may be divisive to the team.

If a team does not deliberately set operating guidelines, then existing norms or habits

> **Operating guidelines**
> Agreements for group interaction that are created and supported by all team members.
>
> **KEY TERM**

become the guidelines by default. Virtual teams may therefore suboptimize their team by incorporating as cultural norms unstated but predictable behavior such as "We'll have the conference calls when they are best for the team members in the main office locations even if they are not convenient for those in the remote locations" or "Preferential treatment will be given to those who have the best English-speaking skills" or "It's okay to display rude behavior online" or "Team members who live closest to the manager will get the best assignments." Most virtual team members would be horrified to see norms like this written down, but they can become common team behavior if they are not challenged and corrected.

> **MINI-CASE: PROBLEMS WITH PERFORMANCE APPRAISALS**
>
> FOR EXAMPLE
>
> One company discovered a strong statistical correlation between performance review results and distance from management, with those who lived farthest from the manager's location getting the lowest scores. Apparently management trusted those they saw most regularly and tended to reward them with the most important elements of the projects, which then resulted in higher performance rankings. It was not until the trend was identified and discussed that it could be replaced with more appropriate (and probably more legal) operating guidelines. The problem might have been avoided if employee concerns about the proper functioning of the virtual teams had been addressed up front with a discussion of operating guidelines.

Ideally, operating guidelines are established while the team is still forming and then continually revised and updated as the team progresses. But it is never too late to create them. A virtual team can be improved by using any of the tools mentioned in this chapter even if the ideal time to use the tool has passed.

> **SETTING (AND CHANGING) OPERATING GUIDELINES**
>
> MISTAKE PROOFING
>
> The power in the operating guideline tool comes because each team member is willing not only to hold herself or himself accountable for the agreements, but they are willing to hold every other team member accountable, as well. People don't do that unless they are fully committed, and that commitment is a function of personal involvement. Each team member must participate and agree to each operating guideline. Among other implications, this means every time the team composition changes, the operating guidelines need to be revisited.

Operating guidelines should relate to all aspects of the team's work, not just meeting behavior. All team members should be involved in setting the operating guidelines. This allows everyone to hold one another accountable for conformance to the agreements.

Operating guidelines, if implemented properly, can be a powerful force for shaping team behavior because they are publicly created and supported agreements on how to work together. In this way they create the virtual team culture and can either substitute for the fragmented and ineffective culture that is common in virtual teams or refocus a less-than-

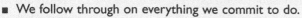

> ## OPERATING GUIDELINES EXAMPLES
>
> Here is an example of one virtual team's operating guidelines:
> - We follow through on everything we commit to do.
> - We keep the team up to date.
> - We always assume good intentions on the part of other team members.
> - If we have an issue with another team member, we will contact him or her personally to discuss the matter.
> - We follow the technology protocols we have established.
> - Customers are our number-one priority. We always make decisions based on what is best for the customer.
> - We use agendas for all meetings, virtual and face-to-face, and send out minutes within two days.
> - We will have a face-to-face meeting at least quarterly.

ideal homogenous culture. One especially important type of operating guideline for a virtual team is what we call technology-use protocols (agreements on how to use collaboration technologies such as e-mail, instant messaging, social networking sites, and Web conferencing).

> **Technology-use protocols** Jointly created agreements on how to use collaboration technologies.   **KEY TERM**

Technology-Use Protocols

We had an interesting discussion one afternoon with salespeople at CDW. After sharing that much of their e-mail work had to be done at home—often consuming as much as six hours of their time *after* a full workday with clients—a disagreement occurred. About half of the group complained that salutations in e-mail (Dear so-and-so) and the obligatory social comments at the beginning of many e-mails (How have you been? It was sure great to see you last Tuesday, etc.) were a colossal waste of time.

The other half thought that jumping right into the work part of the message was rude and unnecessarily cold. While discussing technology-use protocols they decided to eliminate these elements in their correspondence with each other, but if they wouldn't have talked about it, this small difference of opinion would have gone unresolved and perhaps grown into a productivity-wasting conflict.

There are few right answers about technology use other than this: Talk about it! Make a decision! Don't leave part of the group frustrated because of undiscussed issues such as "Why does part of the team answer e-mails on weekends while part does not?" or "How quickly do we have to respond to instant messages?" or "When should we use the telephone instead of e-mail?" or "Is it okay to discuss work on my social networking pages?" or "Why doesn't part of the team write a salutation in work messages?" Without talking about it, violated expectations are inevitable, and otherwise preventable conflict within the team can occur.

THE IMPORTANCE OF JOINTLY CREATED AGREEMENTS

CAUTION

Like other types of operating guidelines, technology-use protocols derive their power from the agreement reached by all the team members. They have little effect on technology use if they are created by management or technical specialists and distributed to the team to implement. Conversely, if they are created and supported by the team as a whole (including management), peer pressure will encourage compliance and discourage variance.

For example, when many of the teams we've worked with discuss how to use e-mail, they agree to abide by a no-scrolling rule (the message should be short enough to fit on one computer screen so that it does not require scrolling) or to check e-mail at least twice each workday. Agreements like this increase productivity and reduce the conflict that can occur from violated expectations.

SAMPLE E-MAIL PROTOCOLS

FOR EXAMPLE

We will clearly identify the subject of the message in the subject line.

- All e-mail messages will be short (no scrolling required) and to the point.
- E-mail will not be used for philosophical debates.
- All distribution lists will be kept current.
- E-mail will not be used for urgent messages.
- We accept responsibility for a personal delivery (face-to-face or voice-to-voice) of any urgent message.
- To enable message prioritization, we will code the top of each message with either "requires action" or "for your information (FYI)."
- We will sign all messages.

- We agree that e-mail is a supplement to, not a substitute for, personal interaction.
- We will not spam.
- We will treat people electronically the same way we would in person.
- Instead of copying long quotes from others, we will briefly summarize them and add attachments, if necessary.

Setting Technology Protocols

These technology-use protocols should be put in place for all types of technology used by the team. They needn't be long, but should be detailed enough to provide clear direction. It's best to be as specific as possible. A voice mail protocol, for example, that states "We won't leave messages longer than 10 seconds" is less open to interpretation and misunderstanding than "We'll only leave brief vm messages."

VOICE MAIL PROTOCOL

- We do not leave messages longer than 10 seconds.
- We check our voice mail at least once a day.
- We use the "urgent" code only when a message is truly urgent.
- We limit the use of the "group send" option. We use it only when a message is relevant to all members.
- When forwarding messages, we will leave an explanatory message so the individual knows why the message is being sent.
- We take accountability to follow up voice mail messages with written documentation when necessary.
- We never use voice mail to leave emotionally charged messages. We wait to talk with the person directly (phone or in person) so the problem or issue can be jointly resolved.

The process of creating technology protocols allows team members to acknowledge and incorporate technology preferences into the way they work. For example, during this discussion it may become clear that Priya prefers e-mails, while Jordan prefers instant messaging, helping everyone understand the best ways to contact each other. These agreements may also help people reduce stress and ensure more effective work/home life balance, as we discuss in later chapters. We also review several collaboration technologies in more detail in later chapters. In those chapters we recommend protocols your team may want to consider for each technology.

Manager's Checklist for Chapter 6

☑ A new virtual team member has to be properly oriented. The sink-or-swim method often used for collocated teams can be especially problematic for virtual teams where people are often working on their own with little guidance from others.

☑ Some of the better activities to consider for an orientation include a face-to-face orientation and team introduction meeting, a history and status review, technology training, a review of the key team tools you use, a discussion of the organization's culture, and a realistic preview of what it means to operate as member of a virtual team.

☑ Some people work well on virtual teams and some don't. Look for demonstrated competencies in areas such as willingness to take accountability for results, good interpersonal skills and judgment, and technological competence in both the technologies necessary to do the work and the ones necessary to communicate effectively with you and the other members of the virtual team. It's especially important to select people who are self-starters and who can work independently without a lot of supervision. But they need to enjoy and be capable of working on a team. How do you know all of these things? Don't ask yes-or-no questions—ask for examples of what they have done before. Probe to see what they like and dislike, and where they have a proven track record of success. And have them talk with other team members. If the team members don't participate in the hiring process, they'll be less likely to train or help the team member later.

☑ Three tools are especially helpful for starting up or refocusing virtual teams: team charters, role clarification processes, and operating guidelines.

☑ These three tools can help virtual teams create a shared work culture that bridges differences and increases clarity and productivity.

☑ The discussion that creates the charter, roles, and agreements is probably more important than the final product. The participation of all team members is critical.

☑ It's important to involve the right people in the chartering process, including people outside the team who have a major impact on the team's ability to be successful, such as key customers or partners and senior management sponsors.

☑ If operating guidelines are not set and agreed to properly, dysfunctional team norms can take their place as a key predictor of team behavior.

☑ Operating guidelines can increase productivity and reduce unhealthy tension among team members.

☑ Technologies such as e-mail, Web conferencing, and instant messaging facilitate virtual team communication, but they can cause impediments to both team and individual effectiveness.

☑ Technology-use protocols can increase productivity and reduce unhealthy tension among team members.

Note

Much of the information in this chapter is excerpted from a workbook we use to train clients entitled *Selecting and Orienting Virtual Team Members* (The Fisher Group, Inc., 2010) and from a chapter in *The Virtual Handbook of High Performance Virtual Teams* (Kimball Fisher, "Tools for Effective Virtual Team Start-Ups," Jossey-Bass, 2008) which excerpts material from a workbook entitled *Virtual Team Start-Ups* (The Fisher Group, Inc., 2006). All are used by permission of the authors and copyright holders.

Chapter
7

Building Trust from a Distance

The leaders who work most effectively, it seems to me, never say "I." And that's not because they have trained themselves not to say "I." They don't think "I." They think "we"; they think "team." They understand their job to be to make the team function. They accept responsibility and don't sidestep it, but "we" gets the credit. This is what creates trust, what enables you to get the task done.
—Peter F. Drucker

A leader's ability to develop trust is crucial. Trust creates greater openness and leads to improved information sharing, problem solving, innovation, action, and commitment. Research indicates that organizations with higher trust have better performance (Dennis Reina and Michelle Reina, *Trust and Betrayal in the Workplace*, Berrett-Koehler, 2006), a correlation that experienced managers have intuited for years.

Building and maintaining trust is difficult in any team, but the issues are especially challenging when the team is spread across multiple locations and the team leader is forced to coach and interact with the team from a distance. In this chapter we examine several key actions that can build or erode trust when working virtually, including general tips that will aid the virtual leader in creating and maintaining a trusting environment. We also review the importance of celebrating achievements and milestones in virtual teams as a trust-building activity.

> **Trust** The individual and organizational condition that fosters risk taking; encourages personal accountability, joint problem solving, conflict resolution, and the free expression of ideas; **KEY TERM** allows the giving and receiving of honest feedback; and prevents blaming, gossiping, and inappropriate criticism. It is a function of effective social communication and experience, normally resulting from getting to know others in the organization not just as co-workers, but as fellow human beings with shared hopes, fears, and commitment to accomplishing the purpose of the team.

To better understand trust issues on virtual teams, consider the following case.

The Problematic E-Mail

Louisa works as an underwriter for Countrywide Insurance. In an effort to streamline the underwriting process, a project team with representatives from each of the company's eight divisions has been formed to look at procedures and workflow. Louisa, from the Dallas branch, has been asked to serve on the team and is looking forward to sharing some of her ideas for improvements.

Thursday morning Louisa logs onto her computer and checks e-mail. She sees a message from Charles, project team leader, who works in the Charlotte branch office. Eager to hear what he has to say about the project, Louisa opens the message and begins to read:

> I wanted to let all members of the Underwriting process improvement team know that I have scheduled a teleconference meeting next Tuesday at 3:00 P.M. East Coast time. Please call 1-889-429-3080 promptly at 2:55 to join the conference.
>
> As project leader I want to share my expectations for the team. I have served on many virtual project teams and they can be very effective or very ineffective. Two things that make a team very ineffective are (1) failure to follow through on assignments and (2) failure to show up for teleconferences.
>
> Since we are all located in different offices around the country and in Canada, teleconferences are our primary means of communication on this project. Therefore, it is important that you contact me at least two days prior to each conference if you are unable to attend. Also, I would like to receive weekly e-mail reports from each of you on the status of

your project assignments.

This is a very important project. The outcome of our work will dictate how the underwriting process is carried out for years to come. Because of its importance, we need full cooperation from every member.

Please be prepared and on time for our Tuesday call.

Best regards,
Charles Morgan

Louisa hated to admit it, but she now had an uneasy feeling in her stomach about the project. The e-mail from Charles made her uncomfortable. It sounded punitive and a little controlling. Didn't he trust the project team members? It sure didn't sound like it.

Case Discussion

In the problematic e-mail case, Charles made some serious, but common, mistakes. How would you feel if you received his message? Trusted? Empowered? Although this case is a compilation of several experiences (and is disguised to avoid embarrassing a few otherwise great managers), it shows how dashing off a quick message—probably in a well-intentioned attempt to provide some quick clarity and demonstrate leadership—backfired. It is likely that if Charles would have waited to send the e-mail until after he read it back to himself carefully, he would have noted the tone of distrust and control. But since he didn't, he now has to undo the damage and rebuild trust in the team.

Tips for Developing Trust

Consider the following tips for building trust across distance.

Tip #1: Be honest. This is perhaps the single most important variable that affects trust. Leaders who demonstrate openness about their actions, intentions, and vision soon find that people respond positively to self-disclosure and sincerity.

Tip #2: From the outset, set the tone for future interaction. The initial actions of the leader set the tone and establish norms and expectations for the team's interactions.

Carefully review all correspondence, checking the overall tone. The first written communication with team members sets a precedent for future interactions and contributes heavily to the team's perceptions of the leader. Consider such things as the terms or words you use. Does the message convey respect for all team members? Is the language inclusive of all cultures and locations? Does the wording reflect your confidence in the team and its ability to work together virtually?

Provide an opportunity for team members to get acquainted before launching into a project or day-to-day work. It's a good idea to invest time in some kind of introductory activity that allows team members to share information about themselves with one another.

Tip #3: To get trust, give trust. Trusting others is the best place to begin in creating an environment of trust. Leaders set the example for the rest of the team. Waiting to give trust to employees until they earn it is never as effective as assuming they are trustworthy unless they prove otherwise.

Tip #4: Communicate openly and frequently. Communication can come in many forms. Consider, for instance, such varied approaches as presentations, periodic newsletters with information pertinent to the team and company, daily voice mail updates, quarterly face-to-face meetings, and/or weekly e-mail summaries of project status.

The key to effective virtual team communication is to never make team members guess what you are thinking, or what is going on with one another. Distance employees tend to believe that no news is bad news, so more frequent contact can help alleviate some of the anxiety that accompanies working virtually.

Tip #5: Do what you say you will do and make your actions visible. Visibly keeping commitments increases trust. Team members pick up quickly on insincere rhetoric or broken promises. While this is true in any team, distance magnifies the impact of a leader's perceived lack of action.

Tip #6: Be accessible and responsive. Obviously, this can be difficult when working across multiple time zones. Find ways to make yourself regularly available to team members. One way to do this is to establish a rotating schedule of in-person visits for each site. Likewise, setting a regular virtual meeting time via teleconference, videoconference, or Web conference, etc., provides team members with the assurance that there will be an opportunity to address questions or problems without a significant waiting period.

When working remotely, team members need to feel the leader is as responsive as he or she would be in a collocated situation. Therefore, it is important that the leader respond to e-mail or voice mail messages within 24 hours. If the issue or question presents an emergency, the leader needs to respond immediately.

If team members are expected to meet established timelines, they will look to the leader to quickly get them answers, resources, information, or approvals. Lack of timely response can look like sabotage to someone sitting thousands of miles away facing a customer demanding an answer. Establish agreements up front on how you will respond to team inquiries or requests and in what time frame. Honor those agreements throughout the life of the project or relationship.

> ## BE TRANSPARENT
>
> Not only is it important to take action, but it is equally critical that you make your actions visible. Instead of assuming that team members know you did something, tell them. Saying something like "In response to your suggestions about such and such, I did such and such yesterday. Thanks for the recommendation" goes a long way in building confidence that you will respond as necessary to maintain team alignment and focus. It's an extra step, and it takes time, but it can be a powerful practice for building trust.

Tip #7: Make sure that interactions with the team are consistent and predictable. The process of building trust is not an event—it is a process. Trust results from predictable interaction over time. If team members see a leader respond one way this week and another way next week, it becomes harder and harder to trust him or her.

Tip #8: Create social time for the team. In collocated teams, much of the trust and confidence that team members have in one another and in the leader come from informal social interaction. For virtual teams to have this experience requires more thought and creativity. Perhaps the easiest way is to build informal socializing time into videoconferences or teleconferences. At either the beginning or the end of a call or meeting, the leader might lead the way with informal conversation, asking about team members' outside interests, families, etc.

DESTROYING TRUST IS EASY
Even though everybody knows it, remember that trust can be destroyed much more easily than it can be created. It can take years to build trust but only moments to ruin it. Keep this sobering thought in mind as you interact with the team. Recovering from a misstatement, unwarranted criticism, or missed opportunity may take months of work.

How Overcoming Isolation in Virtual Teams Builds Trust

Many individuals working virtually experience a sense of isolation, missing the normal day-to-day collegial interaction and business socialization that accompanies typical corporate life. If not addressed, this can have dire consequences for both the individual and the team. Feelings of resentment may begin to surface, leading to the erosion of trust among team members. The experience of successful virtual teams reveals several techniques that can help overcome this isolation and increase trust levels among virtual colleagues.

Provide new team members with thorough training and an in-depth orientation on how to function in a virtual environment. Have other team members who have worked in this team or similar situations share their perspectives, both positive and negative, with the new employee. Assign each new team member a "virtual buddy"—someone who stays in contact with the new employee to answer questions, offer suggestions on working virtually, etc. Set up regular times for them to talk on the phone or communicate via instant messaging.

Use visual reminders of one another. For instance, if the team has the opportunity to meet face-to-face, take a group picture and give all the team members a copy to keep near their computer or telephone as a visual reminder of their teammates. Mementos of a team-building session or videoconference celebration (e.g., a mug or a plaque) can also serve to create a physical sense of "team."

Create "highway cafés." In a collocated environment, the company cafeteria provides a convenient place for teammates to informally network. If the members of a virtual team are located in the same city or within driving distance of one another, they can connect via "highway cafés." Sales

> ## WORKING AT HOME IS NOT FOR THE TIMID
> When Weyerhaeuser first started experimenting with people
> working from home (it was called "telecommuting" back then),
> the company ran into a troubling problem: performance
> dropped. One HR team discovered, for example, that the quality and timeliness of a telecommuter dropped significantly below her previous work
> standard. Hoping it was a temporary problem, the team did nothing. Trust
> eroded as the team assumed that she had become less committed and she
> assumed that the team didn't want to help her be successful. Weeks later
> the telecommuter confessed that she was embarrassed to contact her
> teammates and "interrupt them" by asking clarifying questions about her
> assignment (something she had no problem doing when she shared an
> office with them). They came to realize that they had to find ways to create
> structured interaction opportunities. And the telecommuter learned that
> she needed to be bolder and ask for the things she needed to get her work
> done. After some adjustments they learned how to work virtually, and then
> they shared their learnings with others.

reps from satellite offices, for instance, might agree to meet at a designated restaurant to socialize and share pertinent information. Similarly, a consultant working alone much of the time might schedule regular lunches with virtual co-workers or friends from different companies as a way to maintain human interaction and contact.

Create "cyber cafés" on your company intranet so virtual employees can stay in touch and talk informally. A sanctioned intranet chat room not only reduces the sense of isolation felt by virtual workers; it also fosters creativity across distance. It provides a place for co-workers to meet and exchange ideas, get feedback, share recent learning experiences, and gain a fresh perspective from others.

Use a "hoteling" approach to office space. This is useful when virtual team members are working out of cars or home offices. Employees can call ahead and reserve an office space for the day or for a few hours. This provides at least occasional office interaction. Some organizations make these "hotel" office spaces more personal by providing a wall or other space where team members can display pictures or personal items that might be found in any traditional office.

Create a team Web page. Not only does a team web page provide a place for formal business communication and a storage site for important

SMART

MANAGING

DON'T LOOK OVER THEIR SHOULDERS
Creating a work-related social networking space is tricky. If the employee comments are overly monitored by management, the comments will eventually become less open and useful. Management often has legitimate concerns about exposing trade secrets or allowing inappropriate interaction on a team wiki or intranet, but in these cases it may be better to not make the tool available than to significantly reduce its effectiveness. People understand when harassing, bullying, or other inappropriate comments are deleted or responded to, but if team members feel like Big Brother is watching, they eventually won't use the technology at all. To help with this, many teams create a technology-use protocol to deal with these communications. When *they* self-monitor appropriate social networking communication, management intervention isn't required.

records, but it also creates a sense of shared identity for team members. Put team member photographs on the page and consider having each team member embed a brief video introducing himself or herself (to save bandwidth have the members link to a YouTube piece they created). The team may also want to create a team symbol or graphic, which, like a corporate logo, can provide an additional sense of identity.

Celebrating from a Distance

Celebrating a team's milestones or an individual team member's achievement helps to build a cohesive team and to keep morale and motivation high. These kinds of acknowledgments also help virtual team members feel connected regardless of the distance that separates them.

There are countless ways to carry out successful distance celebrations. Review the following suggestions and then consider what additional ideas you may have for your virtual team.

Celebrate the "small" stuff. Acknowledge personal milestones such as birthdays, anniversaries, weddings, the birth of a child, a recent accomplishment such as completing schooling, or a contribution to a community effort. Although most of these events are not directly related to work, they are a significant part of what makes each of us who we are.

Celebrating such events communicates to each individual that he or she is more than just an impersonal node on your team's network.

Knowing about each other's achievements, however small, helps build camaraderie and respect across distance; and if your team were collocated, the members would probably do this on their own to get to know each other better.

Create a place on your intranet for posting best practices and learnings. The opportunity to share your learnings or to have a process or approach you have designed posted as a best practice is a subtle, but effective, way to acknowledge accomplishments. It not only allows the team or individual to receive recognition, but also enables team members to learn best practices from one another.

Include others in the celebration, whether electronically or face-to-face. For instance, if the team is having a teleconference or videoconference celebration for a fellow team member, invite his or her on-site co-workers to drop by the area where the guest of honor is located and deliver their congratulations during the celebration. Or make a video that includes both on-site co-workers and the virtual team members and attach it to a celebratory e-mail or play it as part of the conference.

Use "portable parties." When the team plans to celebrate special milestones via teleconference or videoconference, put together a "party kit" and send one to each team member. Include things such as party hats, horns,

> **REMEMBER THE CAKE!**
>
> *FOR EXAMPLE*
>
> One of our clients, an attorney who serves as senior counsel for a *Fortune* 100 company, tells the story of how her team celebrated her birthday virtually while she was on a work assignment in Mexico. Although she enjoyed participating in the videoconference with them, she was jealous that they were eating her birthday cake without her. While she enjoyed giving them a hard time about that oversight for months afterward, it really wouldn't have taken much effort or expense to get her a small cake in her remote location.

confetti, party favors, certificates of achievement, or small inexpensive gifts or mementos that represent the project, task, or specific milestone. Ask all the members to bring their kit to the meeting. Do a check to make sure they all have their party supplies. This kind of lighthearted fun can be helpful and healthy, especially if the team has been under a great deal of pressure.

Respect personal preferences when deciding how to celebrate. What may constitute a reward or positive recognition for one individual may be the opposite for another. Some people, for example, may feel embarrassed or uncomfortable if they are singled out for recognition. Also, when there are multiple cultures represented on the team, remember that what is celebratory in one culture may be offensive in another. It's a good idea to ask the individual who is being recognized, or to decide as a team, what celebration activities would be most enjoyable for all.

Include face-to-face celebrations. Where possible, it's a good idea for virtual co-workers to come together at key points during the life of a project or at regularly scheduled intervals. This face-to-face social time helps the team gel and get to know one another more quickly than distance communication alone typically allows. These meetings or get-togethers provide an ideal setting in which to incorporate celebration. For instance, at the beginning of a project the team members can celebrate the inception of the group and/or the project or task they are about to undertake. At the conclusion of the project the team can acknowledge and celebrate its success and mentally prepare to move on to a new assignment.

Celebrate mileposts. Don't limit celebrations to the "big finish." This is especially critical for virtual teams in order to keep motivation and morale high, since individuals can't give one another "high fives" on a daily basis. These don't have to be big events. Some kind of simple recognition that clearly delineates progress will go a long way in letting all team members know that their efforts are paying off and appreciated.

Trust is the lubricant for social interaction. These tips can help you avoid the costly repair work necessary if you lose it.

Manager's Checklist for Chapter 7

☑ Appropriate celebrations and recognitions help a team build trust. Although not all the recommendations listed in this chapter will be right for every team, consider celebrating mileposts (not only major accomplishments), including celebrations in your face-to-face activities, respecting personal celebration preferences, doing "portable parties," including more than just the team members, posting best practices and team accomplishments, and celebrating personal accomplishments like birthdays, weddings, and child-births.

☑ Helping people overcome a feeling of isolation builds trust. Useful practices for this include creating team Web pages to foster team identity and collaboration space, "hoteling" and/or creating "cyber cafés" or "highway cafés" to promote team member interaction, using visual reminders to help team members remember that they are part of something bigger than themselves, and conducting high-quality orientations to train people on effective teaming.

☑ Tips for building trust include creating social time for the team, making sure that interactions are predictable and consistent, being accessible and responsive, doing what you said you would do (and making your actions visible), communicating openly and frequently, acting as though people are trustworthy, taking the extra effort to use a trusting tone in communicating via technology, and being honest. In later chapters we deal with the problems of overcommunication, but as far as trust is concerned, it's better to err on the side of over-communication than undercommunication.

☑ Trust is a function of predictable interaction over time. It doesn't come quickly, but can be destroyed easily. The best course of action is to avoid trust-eroding interactions so you don't have to lose the ground you have worked so hard to build.

Note

Much of this information is from our book *The Distance Manager*, which excerpts a workbook entitled *Managing Trust from a Distance* (The Fisher Group, Inc., 2000), which we use to train clients. Used by permission of the authors and copyright holders.

Using Telephonic Collaboration Technologies

It is my heart-warmed and world-embracing Christmas hope and aspiration that all of us, the high, the low, the rich, the poor, the admired, the despised, the loved, the hated, the civilized, the savage (every man and brother of us all throughout the whole earth), may eventually be gathered together in a heaven of everlasting rest and peace and bliss, except the inventor of the telephone.

—Mark Twain
Christmas greeting, 1890

Even basic communication tools have to be managed effectively or they can worsen virtual team effectiveness by increasing confusion, becoming an interruption (instead of a facilitation) of work, and resulting in a significant waste of time. It's easy to grow to despise the collaborative technologies that should be making our lives easier, if they aren't producing that result.

To introduce this chapter consider the following case.

Mini-Case Study: A Day in the Life of a Virtual Team Leader

As Camille wakes up, she glances at her smartphone and notices that she has five new voice mails. "Well, looks like a typical morning," she thinks as she sits up in bed. "Which should I do first, check the voice mail messages or wade my way through my e-mails?"

For the past two months, Camille has been the team leader of a company design team that has members spread across five countries. It has been a real challenge to keep the team working together and focused on the same goals and issues. In particular, Camille struggles to ensure that the team receives timely and accurate communication.

Camille checks and discovers that she has 28 e-mail messages—and it's only 5:30 A.M.! The first three e-mails are from the engineer in Germany and consist of irrelevant updates on topics that only the German contingent needs to know. "Geèz, these guys copy the team on everything!" Camille laments. "And here's one from the St. Louis rep with the same problem. The team will never complete the component design if they have to read every update on every issue." After checking her messages, she pops into the shower, grabs a power bar for breakfast, and then drives to her office in the Silicon Valley.

As she walks in, her desk phone rings, and she remembers that the team has a teleconference scheduled for 8 A.M. "Oh, is it already time for the project team conference call?" Camille wonders to herself. "I hope everyone makes it this time. Last week the engineers from Singapore and Japan blew off the meeting because of when it was scheduled."

As Camille picks up the phone she hears the voices of Stefan from Germany, Rick and Serena from Seattle, Hideo and Tomako from Tokyo, and Carlos from Spain. "Hi, everyone," Camille says. "Are we all here? I don't hear Wai Ho from the Singapore office or Mark from the New Jersey office. Are they planning to join us?"

"I doubt it," says Rick. "Mark mentioned that he had a lunch date with a customer." He then texts Camille on her cell phone. "Wai Ho said he needed sleep more than another meeting."

As the meeting progresses with each site reporting its status, an annoying thumping noise keeps interfering with Camille's ability to hear what is being said. Finally she asks, "What is that noise? Can the rest of you hear it?"

"Oh, sorry," says Serena. "I was tapping my pencil on the table and didn't realize it was near the microphone."

The meeting wraps up about 11 A.M. West Coast time. "Well done, everybody," Camille says. "Let's meet this same time next week."

Camille plows her way through the rest of her e-mail and heads out for lunch.

At 1:00 Camille joins a Skype video teleconference with Mark, Rick, and Serena. Rick is describing how the component gauge will work and how he has eliminated one of the problem switches to make the design simpler. Most of the meeting is a one-way lecture from Rick, with others adding the occasional comment. He never uses any presentation slides, photos, or drawings. Camille quickly finds her mind wandering as she thinks about what to do about Wai Ho. Should she call him and confront him about skipping the teleconference again? She suddenly realizes that she just missed about 10 minutes of Rick's lecture, but is too embarrassed to make him repeat what he already said. Finally, at 4:00 P.M. West Coast time, Mark texts everyone that he has to go. "It's 7:00 P.M. here and I really have to go. Thanks for the update, Rick. Looks good!" With that he signs off and the other three are left to wrap things up. Camille suggests that they finish the call tomorrow and asks Rick to set it up and let her know when it will be.

Camille makes one more pass through her e-mails and then decides to call it a day. "Whew," she sighs. "This virtual management stuff is tough! Maybe it will get better with time. It's just that with all this communicating we don't have a lot of time to get this project completed. Well, I'll give it another go tomorrow and hope for the best."

Using Communication Technologies Effectively

As this case illustrates, leading a virtual team requires clear, forthright, constant, and effective communication. But there are good ways and bad ways to use collaboration technologies. In this chapter we suggest ways to derive maximum benefit from the most basic of communication technologies—telephony. We discuss telephone-based interactions including telephone calls, teleconferences, and instant messaging (IM). We also briefly mention videophones. In the next chapter we continue the discussion by reviewing tips for videoconferencing and Internet-based technologies such as Web conferencing, whiteboards, and social networking.

TECHNOLOGIES CHANGE

CAUTION Technologies change so rapidly that unless you purchase this book within a few months of publication, it is impossible for it to be current or to include all the key technologies you may be using. But even if the team members aren't expert on a particular technology that comes out after publication of this book, they will learn as a group how it affects them after they use it together. Just remember to talk about it. Do what works. And remember to keep revising your technology-use protocols so they are always up to date.

Effective Phone Use

In spite of all the collaboration technology at our disposal today, the telephone remains a primary means of communication for those working across space and time. And with the advent of the cell and satellite phone, it is now possible to contact almost anyone from almost anywhere.

The telephone is such a familiar part of daily life, however, that we sometimes take it for granted and don't manage its use as well as we should. The suggestions below can help you and those you lead better utilize the telephone as a primary means of communication with virtual teammates. They are simple, commonsense tips that are often overlooked in our rush to get the work done.

Telephone Tips

Use a headset or earbuds. Carrying on a lengthy conversation while taking notes, looking through papers and other materials, or working on a computer whiteboard requires a hands-free process that is ergonomically sound. Unless there are multiple people using one phone, avoid the speakerphone function, because it picks up too much background noise.

Demonstrate phone courtesy. Almost all issues associated with communication get amplified from a distance. This is true of phone manners, too. A few phone etiquette reminders include:

- *Pay attention to the conversation.* Avoid "listener drift"—that process of reflecting on issues other than the one being discussed. This takes a great deal of discipline, because not having eye contact or being able to read body language typically makes it more difficult to concentrate.

- *Be sensitive to voice volume.* Keep your voice low enough that those in your home, the airport, or the surrounding work area aren't disturbed, but loud enough so that those on the line can clearly hear. You know how irritating it is to be at a coffee shop and hear someone's entire conversation. And in days when security concerns are common, make sure that company confidential information is never discussed where it could be overheard. One of the authors was once shocked to hear elements of a company strategic plan on an airplane. This kind of information in the hands of a competitor or unscrupulous businessperson could cause very serious damage to your organization.

- *Avoid talking over others.* This tends to happen more frequently in phone conversations because we don't have the advantage of body language to cue us that the other individual is getting ready to say something. If you do cut others off, apologize and offer to let them complete their thought.

- *When calling unannounced, ask the person if now is a good time to talk.* Don't assume someone is free to take the call right then. For longer conversations, schedule ahead of time just as you would a face-to-face meeting. This is especially important for videophone or computer telephone calls that use a camera. Give people a chance to check their hair and get the spinach out of their teeth before you commit them to a long and distracting call.

Return phone calls in a timely way. If the virtual team has an operating guideline outlining what "timely" means, honor that guideline.

Minimize interruptions. Find a way to let others in your office know that you're on the phone and can't be disturbed. Something as simple as leaving a note on the door saying you are on the phone and can't be disturbed will keep distractions to a minimum. Include a space on the sign for people to leave messages, or hang a sticky pad by the sign so they can jot you a note. This is especially important if you work at home when your kids are there. Have a way to signal them when quiet is important. Remember that this discussion with your kids or roommates should occur before the telephone call (not during it).

Respect time zones. When the team includes individuals from multiple time zones, establish protocols about appropriate times to call. Make sure that everyone gets the opportunity to get up in the middle of the night for teleconferences, rather than limiting that requirement to a few team members.

Also, respect people's personal time. It is best to avoid frequently scheduling calls that require individuals to come in early or stay well past the close of their workday. While this is to be expected on an occasional basis, doing so too often can burn people out.

Use visual information to increase clarity. A complex conversation is greatly enhanced via the use of pictures, diagrams, or text. A discussion regarding a parts problem, for instance, is more effective if all those in the conversation have a drawing of the part. Use your camera on the phone if it will help the conversation, or send any written information ahead of time to reduce questions or confusion. Be certain that all written documents have page numbers. Referencing a page number is easier than trying to describe which page you're on and then waiting for others to catch up.

Set protocols for telephone, voice mail, and instant messaging/texting. If the team hasn't already done so, this is an important step to take. Like other forms of electronic communication, telephone-based communication can run amok. Sometimes it's the simplest technologies that get most often overlooked and, consequently, are used most ineffectively. (See the sidebar "Setting Telephone-Based Protocols" for specific recommendations.)

> **TRICKS OF THE TRADE**
>
> **KEEPING THEM INFORMED**
> Looking for a quick and consistent way to keep people informed? Consider this. One of the virtual team managers we met at the IRS uses a daily voice mail to keep the attorneys and auditors on her team up to date. The voice mails are less than a couple of minutes, and remind people of upcoming events, the latest news, and time-sensitive information. Because the message is brief and practical, team members appreciate and depend on the regular morning message.

When using a phone in the car, always go hands free! Don't endanger yourself or others.

Finally, respect others' voice mail time. Avoid leaving very lengthy or detailed messages. Instead, briefly explain the nature of the call and request that the individual call you back to discuss the details.

SETTING TELEPHONE-BASED PROTOCOLS

SMART

MANAGING

To set these protocols, it is useful for the virtual team to answer a few questions pertaining to this technology. These questions might include:

- What will we use telephones for?
- What topics/decisions/problems should be reserved for Web conferences or face-to-face meetings? Why?
- Who will moderate the calls? Does it always have to be the manager?
- Will notes be kept? By whom?
- What will we use voice mail for? What will we not use it for?
- What will we use IM for? What will we not use it for?
- How long should messages be?
- Will we need to check work voice mail and IMs on weekends, holidays, and vacations?
- How quickly will we commit to responding to messages?
- Do we need to create a way to designate message priorities (urgent, FYI, etc.)?
- In what instances do we need to transfer messages from one voice mailbox to another?
- Is there a special protocol for transfers (e.g., can we just transfer, or do we need to leave an explanatory message)?

Effective Teleconferencing

In spite of the fact that more sophisticated technologies are widely available, at the time of this writing, teleconferencing has become an almost universal method of communication for conducting business from a distance. Many companies, in fact, use teleconferences in place of face-to-face meetings even when the participants are located nearby (e.g., different buildings, same city) to save travel time and reduce their carbon footprint. But often those who participate in teleconferences complain that it just doesn't seem to get the job done as well as face-to-face meetings. See the tips below on making teleconferences more productive.

Tips for Effective Teleconferences

Be certain that the teleconference is well organized. Teleconferences can't be conducted "on the fly"; they require considerable forethought and planning. Those who use teleconferences regularly and successfully affirm that these meetings require greater amounts of preparation than a face-to-face session. All the "rules" and guidelines for conducting effective meetings need to be strictly followed when teleconferencing. One such guideline is to have an agenda and send it out to all participants in advance of the teleconference. This allows those involved to come to the conversation prepared with information, research, documents, etc., that will be required to make the most effective use of time.

Assign meeting roles. One helpful role is that of the "phone leader." The role of the phone leader is to ensure that everyone has equal opportunity to speak. In a face-to-face meeting, "body language" often serves to cue participants that someone wishes to speak. Without that visibility, member contributions can get lost.

One idea is for the phone leader to keep a list of participants' names in front of him or her. During the conference call the leader can place a check by each individual's name as he or she participates, and solicit input from those who haven't had an opportunity to speak.

Use people's names. Without seeing other participants, it's sometimes difficult to know who is speaking. This results in confusion both in the meeting and afterward as people try to figure out who said what or who took which assignments. It's also a help to the scribe so he or she can accurately record assignments. At the start of the teleconference, have members at each site introduce themselves, then set the guideline that individuals will identify themselves each time they speak. Also, when responding to someone else's comment or question, use the person's name.

One gatekeeper we worked with (see the list of virtual meeting roles) had name tents made up for each participant whether the participant was on-site or not. Having a name tent at an open chair for each off-site participant made it easier to remember that there were other people in the meeting who needed to be included and who didn't have the advantage of being within viewing distance of others.

Remember that silence is not consent. Without visual stimulation to keep participants engaged, it's easy to check out or to abdicate ownership for decisions the group makes. Make sure everyone voices his or her concerns and consent before closing on a decision.

Demonstrate good manners. Rudeness is magnified many times over when you aren't face-to-face. It is useful for the phone leader to send out communication guidelines prior to the meeting. These might include tips such as:

- Be on time for the call.
- Don't hold sidebar conversations with people at your site while others are talking from other sites.
- Don't multitask. If you're texting someone or checking e-mails during the conference, your attention is divided.
- Avoid rifling through papers located next to the speakerphone.
- Use the mute button if you aren't talking.
- Stay alert and pay attention.
- Listen carefully to avoid talking over others.

Watch out for background sounds. It's distracting to hear music, nose blowing, throat clearing, eating noises, or background conversations.

VIRTUAL MEETING ROLES

TRICKS OF THE TRADE

Regardless of the communication technology used, when more than two people are having a virtual meeting, it is wise to use meeting roles such as the ones listed below to provide meeting organization and structure. Rotating the roles teaches people that the effective management of a meeting is not the exclusive role of the manager.

- Scribe—Keeps notes for the meeting and distributes them afterward. They include key decisions made, information shared, and action items that require follow-up.
- Gatekeeper—Watches the gate of participation and opens it to those who haven't participated and closes it to those who have had a disproportionate amount of speaking time. This can be done by saying something like, "Thanks for your input, Mary. Jane, what are your concerns?"
- Leader—Prepares the meeting and facilitates it. By paying attention to the agenda, the leader can make certain that the most important parts of the agenda are covered in the allotted time.
- Participant—Comes prepared to the meeting, honestly expresses his or her views, respects others, supports group decisions, etc.

When it comes to using the telephone, don't let your familiarity with a well-known collaboration technology lull you into ineffective communication and interaction.

Instant Messaging

IM can be either phone- or Internet-based, but we discuss it in this chapter as a phone technology. As IM has become more popular, its downside has become obvious. In a recent meeting with senior executives from a large corporation, for example, we witnessed most of the executives responding to IMs during the discussion of a critical business strategy. At the end of the meeting when facilitators reviewed the list of strategic decisions, several executives looked startled and said that they couldn't support them. When the facilitators asked why they hadn't surfaced these important objections when the decisions were being discussed instead of at the end of the meeting, they sheepishly admitted that they had been distracted by important IMs and hadn't been paying enough attention to the meeting.

What texting-crazy high school students have known for years is now becoming obvious to businesspeople. You can't pay attention to your virtual-world technology and your real-world circumstances at the same time. In high school, the worst-case scenario is that these distractions can ruin relationships (picture a young man on a date texting one young woman while having dinner with another) or cause accidents (texting or Twittering while driving).

The same is true in a business setting. Agreements need to be made about when it is all right to unplug and pay attention to the more immediate face-to-face issues at hand. This also requires an acceptance of the fact that there are times when a team member won't be able to respond immediately. Since many organizations have at least brief periods where team members must be available for safety, emergency, or other factors like customer responsiveness, this issue must be discussed.

Videophones

Although moderately priced phones with video technologies are now widely available, we discuss the majority of the concerns with video camera meeting use in the next chapter when we review video and Web conferencing. At this point we simply mention a caution everybody knows, but still sometimes forgets: You're on camera! Don't do anything you wouldn't want projected onto TV sets across the country.

Technologies are meant to serve us, but if we don't use them properly, even basic telephony tools do little more than provide a distraction from work.

Manager's Checklist for Chapter 8

☑ IMs require agreement on when it's OK to unplug. Be especially careful not to let the technology distract you when you're in the middle of a rare opportunity to have a face-to-face interaction with a team member or business associate.

☑ A virtual meeting needs a lot of good preparation and facilitation. Teleconferences benefit from techniques to keep people highly engaged in the interactions. Even a highly interactive virtual meeting, however, is unlikely to keep people's attention for more than two hours.

☑ Remember to use names on teleconferences. Basic courtesy helps a lot on the phone. And if your call (or meeting) uses cameras, don't do anything on camera you wouldn't want projected onto a building in Times Square.

Note

Much of this information is from our book *The Distance Manager*, which excerpted a workbook entitled *Using Communication Technologies Effectively* (The Fisher Group, Inc., 2000) that we use to train clients. Used by permission of the authors and copyright holders.

Chapter 9

Using Videoconferencing and Internet-Based Collaboration Tools

Lo! Men have become the tools of their tools.
—Henry David Thoreau

n the last chapter, we introduced the general challenges associated with collaborative technologies and reviewed telephone-based tools. In this chapter we review the technologies we believe made virtual teams possible: Internet-based tools such as e-mail, Web conferencing, and social networking. These technologies are particularly susceptible to proliferation and abuse, and we can't blame virtual team members if they sometimes feel they are serving the collaboration tools instead of feeling that the tools serve them.

We'd like to start, however, with a non-Internet technology that has been around for a long time but didn't get much traction until the introduction of what experts call "telepresence" platforms. After reviewing videoconferencing—the newly resuscitated tool for virtual team collaboration—we discuss the Internet tools.

Videoconferencing

Once video technology evolved to the point where people could see near-life-size video images simulating a face-to-face meeting environment (supplemented with the ability to use PowerPoint-type computer presentations and microphone-activated cameras to switch to whoever was

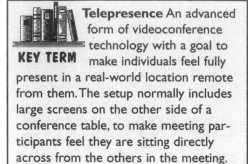

Telepresence An advanced form of videoconference technology with a goal to **KEY TERM** make individuals feel fully present in a real-world location remote from them. The setup normally includes large screens on the other side of a conference table, to make meeting participants feel they are sitting directly across from the others in the meeting.

speaking), it became a viable option for virtual collaboration. Gone, finally, were the days of squinting at a 36" screen trying to see the facial expressions of a few bored-looking teammates as you had a telephone-quality conversation with them. But using a technology with cameras has its own special challenges.

Problems with Meetings with Cameras

Consider this true scenario that took place in a *Fortune* 100 company. A videoconference was set up to interview a potential vendor for an upcoming project. Participants included representatives from four sites, in addition to the vendor representatives and some staff members at the company corporate headquarters.

The conference started well. Video pictures were clear from each of the remote sites as the people from various locations introduced themselves and asked a series of questions to which the vendors responded. The participants were well prepared for the conference, and the meeting was well organized and facilitated by a staff member at the headquarters site.

After the initial question-and-answer period with each site, the vendors made a brief presentation. The host organization's technology then automatically rotated the pictures on the monitor so that each site was highlighted in turn. This allowed the vendors to watch the responses of the remote sites during their presentation. When three of the video pictures came on the screen, small groups of employees were seen nodding their heads and listening attentively. But the fourth video feed was different. A woman who was the single representative of her organization started eating lunch on camera. When her video came on screen, there were distracting noises as she shuffled and crumpled her plastic and paper bags. She looked at her food instead of at the camera and began vigorously scratching her nose. The facilitator, afraid to embarrass the woman by saying something, remained silent. Although the picture lasted only a few moments, other conference participants, including the vendors, found it difficult to keep their train of thought. We were the vendors. It was awful.

Effective Videoconferencing

Consider the following tips:

Use the applicable tips from the previous chapter on teleconferencing. Like teleconferences, videoconferences require excellent preparation and facilitation.

Remember that you're on camera. Don't do anything during a videoconference you wouldn't do on live television. Technology can amplify problems many times. Things that might be acceptable in face-to-face meetings (eating, shuffling papers, moving around) can be problematic in videoconferencing. Keep in mind that it's possible that the camera could be doing a dramatic close-up of you at any time If your technology allows you to see yourself, check it out, but don't stare at yourself all of the time. It's rude.

Fill up the video frame. Stay close to the camera. As one manager told us, "Nobody wants to see some miniature face in the corner of the screen."

Don't limit yourselves to talking heads. Take advantage of the full potential of this technology. Don't just talk about something—demonstrate it. For instance, you might show video shorts from the company president's last speech, or take a video camera into the field and show someone actually closing a sale with a customer or tearing apart a pump. A picture is only worth a thousand words if it's the right picture.

Use the mute feature when you aren't talking. Microphones can be sensitive. If you're in a portion of the conference where there isn't interactivity, muting your mic can eliminate unnecessary noise.

Limit videoconferences to a maximum of two hours. The temptation is often to use a videoconference the same way as a face-to-face meeting. But it takes much greater concentration to participate in videoconferences. Participants tire more rapidly and are less attentive after a shorter time than in face-to-face meetings.

Give participants as much control over the technology as possible. For example, find ways to let them zoom in on a particular person rather than be limited to a static view. Create as much interactivity as possible within the technological constraints you have.

Respect people's privacy. Some employees fear that videoconferencing technologies will be used to monitor their work remotely like the security systems in retail stores. Not only does this create distrust and erode morale, but it also causes people to avoid using the technology.

TELEPRESENCE OPTIONS
TOOLS If the cost of telepresence offered by companies like Cisco is prohibitive, we recommend you consider Web conferencing solutions. Skype-type video calls are inexpensive, but at the time of this writing, too low-bandwidth for conversations requiring higher-resolution video. Companies like WebEx, Microsoft, and Google offer other reasonably priced Web conferencing solutions for presentations and good interactivity tools.

At the time of this writing, telepresence setups are still fairly expensive, but they provide such a significantly improved meeting experience over the previous videoconferencing technology as to render the older approach obsolete.

Now let's look at Internet-based communication technologies starting with the oldest (and often maligned): e-mail.

Using E-Mail—Without Letting It Take Over Your Life

Information technology is a two-edged sword. The availability of so much information can cause overload and frustration. Therefore, finding ways to manage data that allows you and all other virtual team members to have the information needed to be effective—without having more than is necessary—is vital.

Following are a number of tips about how to reduce e-mail overload. These will undoubtedly require group discussion and possibly some training. Some may also require you to use (or eliminate) certain features in your e-mail software.

Check e-mail regularly. This prevents a pile-up of messages and eliminates the tedium associated with reading through 30 or 40+ messages at a sitting.

Keeping up on e-mail correspondence also prevents issues from escalating into larger concerns that may require phone calls, teleconferences, video meetings, or face-to-face meetings, all of which negate the timesaving advantages of e-mail.

Use the description line well. This allows people to determine the urgency and relevance of an e-mail message. Some teams establish a coding system that helps people determine whether something requires immediate attention or not. Others try to put the entire message in the description line with E.O.M. (end of message) afterward. If all you have to say is that Thursday's meeting was changed to Tuesday, do an E.O.M.

Have a "no-scrolling" rule. A number of companies use this rule for e-mail—"If it's more than a screen-page-length, it's too long." Messages that are brief and tightly focused save time for both the sender and the recipient.

Avoid group replies. An astute manager in a large multinational company captured the thoughts of people across the globe when he said: "The single biggest improvement we could make in this company to increase productivity would be to disable the group reply button on e-mail!"

> ### NO SCROLLING
>
> One of our clients uses a no-scrolling rule to keep e-mails short. That's not so unusual. What is unusual is that the employees use a smartphone as the reference screen. That makes people get to the point quickly!

Group replies require an enormous amount of time on the part of the receiver to scroll through the mailing list just to find the message. Using group replies also means that countless numbers of people receive copies of documents they may not need, thus clogging the e-mail system with useless information. A worst-case scenario is when an individual gets caught in a written debate in which he or she has little or no interest.

Keep group lists up to date. Reach team agreement on how to keep group lists current. Then, in the event a group reply is necessary, only those who really need the message will receive it.

Don't leave everyone's attachments or full dialog on e-mail replies. Quote only the portions from previous messages that have relevance. If the attachment is no longer useful, delete it. Spending a minimum amount of time on the sending end can save cumulative hours on the receiving end.

Have a "no-spam" rule. Spam is more than unsolicited advertising. It is anything that is unwanted. This is defined by the receiver, not the sender. Often, team members like to send out jokes and cute stories to the team, but this can be time consuming for the reader. While it may at times be difficult to strike the right balance, it's essential that each team member strive to send out enough information to help other team members do their jobs without sending so much that we unintentionally prohibit them from doing their jobs. How do we know how much is too much? Ask. This can be a particularly helpful discussion when establishing e-mail protocols.

Never write something in an e-mail that is private or confidential. Today, many teams are working across organizational lines, sometimes dealing with sensitive information from other companies partnering on a project. This calls for extra effort to ensure that confidentiality is never breached and that corporate-sensitive information is treated with the utmost respect. Assume that anything written in an e-mail will someday show up on the front page of a national newspaper. If that makes you nervous, use a different method to deliver your message. Remember too, that deleted e-mails can often be recovered from your hard drive. Don't assume it's gone because you threw it away.

Avoid putting emotional content into e-mail. If you're feeling emotional when writing an e-mail, it's a good idea to send it to yourself before you send it to the other person. Don't read it until the next day. If you read it later and it still seems OK, then send it. But if you think, "What was I thinking when I wrote that!" start over.

Also, be especially cautious when communicating in teams that cross cultures. What is funny in one culture, for instance, may easily be offensive to another. Stick to using clear business language to avoid misunderstanding. Avoid jokes.

Never use e-mail to address interpersonal issues. Conflict, misunderstand-

> ## Use the Right Tool
>
> Remember that just because technology allows you to do something doesn't mean you should do it. Some things, like potentially emotional conflict resolution, terminations, and certain types of constructive feedback, are still better delivered face-to-face. One engineer told us, for example, that he had been discouraged when he received his annual performance review via e-mail. He had no opportunity to discuss it, ask for examples, or provide his perspective/disagreement. "The worst part," he said, "is that my manager is located in the cubicle right next to mine."
>
> Even in places where some of the team are collocated, communicating via these technologies becomes so habitual that busy people sometimes forget to think about whether the technology they have selected is the right one for the message they need to convey.

ing, miscommunication, etc., are much better handled face-to-face, via phone, or by video. Resolving interpersonal issues typically requires some concentrated, two-way, synchronous effort, to assure that all parties have been heard and understood.

Web Conferencing

Like other distance technologies, Web meetings require more effective planning and facilitation than their face-to-face counterparts. There should be a clear set of objectives and an agenda for each meeting. This helps the facilitator keep the meeting on track.

Two keys to effective Web meetings are (1) keep the length of the meetings short (no longer than two hours), and (2) ind ways to create active involvement in the meetings. It's hard enough to pay attention in a Web meeting when you have a responsibility as a leader, scribe, or gatekeeper. But it is almost humanly impossible to be

> ## Respect Privacy
> Respect privacy—especially in instances when using Webcams with people who work at home. Video or Web conferencing is more intrusive than nonvideo teleconferencing and may require more preparation on the part of the remote parties (e.g., getting cleaned up, fixing up the room where the camera is located, making sure children are taken care of). Make sure all parties have plenty of warning before a conference.

attentive in a Web meeting where you spend most of your time quietly listening to long presentations while you gaze at the computer.

Create excuses for interaction using techniques such as polling, surveys, and discussion periods. As frequent Webinar leaders, we find it helpful to keep a list of participant names and to randomly ask someone from the list to respond to a question about every five minutes. We might ask, "Carlos, if you were the customer, how would you want our team to respond to the concern we were just discussing," or "Mary, we heard Robert's opinion, but where do you stand on this issue?" If people know

SMART MANAGING

TIPS FOR WEB MEETINGS

Engage as many senses as you can. Having everyone watch a presentation together is good, but doing it while they write IM comments to each other is better. Still better is adding audio teleconferencing for real-time discussions or incorporating video. For instance, a camera could be used to point at someone who's having a technical problem with some software so people can help troubleshoot it real time.

Another good idea is to prepare short video clips and incorporate them into a presentation. This is especially effective for things like product demonstrations.

Record meetings for absent members. Distance teams often have difficulty finding a time when all team members can meet. Recorded meetings shouldn't be a regular substitution for personal involvement, but it's better than nothing. It's also helpful for people whose first language is not the language in which the meeting was held. They can review the meeting later at their own speed to increase their comprehension of the proceedings.

Manage the logistics. Make sure all the participants know where the meeting is, how long it will last, and what assignments they may need to complete prior to and after the meeting. Check other details, as well, such as technology compatibility.

Do a quick technology check at the beginning of each meeting. Do a quick test of the different technologies that will be used during the meeting. For instance, if a polling feature will be used during the meeting, ask the individual sites to test this by asking a sample question to get their responses. Also, make sure that all the team members can hear or that they make the necessary adjustments if they can't. Remember that there are still parts of the world where it's difficult to get reliable high-speed connections. You might be explaining the sixteenth slide of your presentation, while two of your team members are looking at slide number thirteen.

they may be called at random to offer an opinion, they are more likely to pay attention and avoid multitasking. But be aware that this approach won't work in cultures where it may be humiliating to call on someone who hasn't volunteered.

Using Whiteboards

Electronic whiteboards are another Web tool that facilitates team interaction. They are a computer version of the erasable whiteboards used by collocated teams to record notes from team meetings or to make drawings.

These two suggestions, if followed, can make whiteboard discussions more effective:

Have a protocol for how to change shared graphics. If, for example, you have interactive whiteboard capability, is it OK for anyone to erase and revise a portion of a graphic, or do you need to talk about it first? Do you want everyone to have the "power of the pen," or will you take turns being the person who revises?

Use whiteboards like a chart pad. Instead of falling into the trap of everyone leaving a meeting with his or her own interpretation of a group decision, for example, have the scribe write notes down on the whiteboard. Then ask, "Is this what we agreed to?" and get a response from each person.

During group activities like brainstorming, the whiteboard provides a public display of people's ideas as they are created, which is essential to making the process work. Whiteboards also provide a process for capturing and getting agreement on all assignments made during the meeting.

Social Networking

With the advent of Internet sites such as Facebook and Twitter, businesses soon saw the benefits of social networking. One of the early popular adaptations of this idea was a proliferation of job-hunting sites, quickly followed by sites like LinkedIn for work-related networking. These sites often provide opportunities for people to get to know their virtual team members better and discuss basic business issues. But there is a downside. Although many organizations use these types of public forums, security concerns prohibit most operations from detailed work-related discussions over the open Internet. Even seemingly innocuous comments about work such as "I talked to (customer) today" or "I'm working on (name of project or process)" can unwittingly telegraph information that may cause competitive damage to the organization.

Many operations, therefore, have employed internal wikis, intranets, or team Web pages (and shared drives to a lesser extent), to access some of the many benefits of social networking behind the relative safety of a company firewall. Primary concerns around these internal-use technologies relate to appropriate monitoring. If there isn't a way to review and delete conversations on a site, for example, cyberbullying, harassment, pornography, and other problems can occur. But overmonitoring by management, as we have mentioned before, makes it unlikely that team members will open up and share some of their most important tacit learnings with each other. It's a difficult tightrope to walk.

If you can find the balance, however, rich opportunities for team identification, shared learning, best practice sharing, training, joint problem solving, and decision making become possible. On the administrative end, these technologies require a lot of upkeep. Some of the biggest challenges for private social networking include a way to remove obsolete material, as well as a way to identify the most correct version of a shared document (it may not always be the document with the latest date, if more recent corrections/additions, for example, were not agreed to by the team).

Does this mean that you shouldn't use public social networking sites? Of course not. Some sales and marketing organizations, in fact, require that team members be actively engaged in building an online presence to create appropriate "buzz" for their organizations and their products and services. Lots of managers maintain blogs and vlogs (video logs) to keep team members up to date on appropriate aspects of the business.

Some types of organizations (both private and public) simply can't prosper without taking advantage of this important marketing channel. But technology-use protocols for social networking sites are especially important. Organizations need to decide what can be discussed online publicly and what cannot. Most teams find that they also need to separate personal from business online presence, including making joint decisions about which sites they will allow customers and business colleagues on and which they will not. The last thing you want is to have a business relationship sour because of something that was seen on a team member's personal social networking page.

Manager's Checklist for Chapter 9

☑ Challenges with social networking activities (including internal sites like wikis, intranets, and team Web pages) include appropriate monitoring and handling of the administrative responsibilities of keeping a site up to date. The use of public social networking sites requires special technology-use protocols to avoid causing big problems.

☑ A virtual meeting needs a lot of good preparation and facilitation. Web conferences (like teleconferences) benefit from techniques to keep people highly engaged in the interactions. Even a highly interactive virtual meeting, however, is unlikely to keep people's attention for more than two hours.

☑ E-mail is tricky. Doing things like avoiding group replies, keeping distribution lists current, and using the subject line well helps a lot. Many people use a "no-scrolling rule" to keep e-mails short.

☑ Most of all, use common sense. You know that every technology has its own strengths and weaknesses. Use the right tool for the right job in the right way.

Note

Much of this information is from our book *The Distance Manager*, which excerpted a workbook entitled *Using Communication Technologies Effectively* (The Fisher Group, Inc., 2010) that we use to train clients . Used by permission of the authors and copyright holders.

Chapter
10

Improving the Business IQ of Team Members

We don't accomplish anything in this world alone . . . and whatever happens is the result of the whole tapestry of one's life and all the weavings of individual threads from one to another that creates something.

—Sandra Day O'Connor

everal years ago, in an article entitled "Substitutes for Hierarchy" (*Organizational Dynamics*, Summer 1988), prolific management writer Edward Lawler introduced the idea that highly empowered teams required not the elimination of hierarchy and management, but different processes (such as education and training, technical controls, and real-time information) as a substitute for them. This idea may be more important today than it was when it was at the time it was introduced. As a leader of a virtual team, you need a variety of these substitutions for hierarchy. One of the most important is business knowledge.

Virtual team members with a high business IQ require less supervision because they are less likely to make decisions or take actions that harm the business. Although team members with lower business understanding are seldom malicious in this regard, their ignorance of business issues such as customer requirements, competitive realities, and the costs of doing business, can lead to incorrect priorities or diminished success. In this chapter we discuss the types of business knowledge virtual team members need, including an understanding of what business they are in, basic economics, who their customers are, and what their customers expect. We also suggest a process for using that knowledge to improve the team's operations.

Understanding Your Business

A good place to start is to engage the virtual team in a discussion of what business it is in. The answer to this question may not be as obvious as it first appears. But answering this question properly is vital to creating and sustaining a successful business.

TRICKS OF THE TRADE

DISCUSSING BUSINESS

To engage a virtual team in a discussion about its business, try one of the following:

- Lead a discussion in a regularly scheduled teleconference.
- Lead a whiteboard discussion. Ask the team the question and then ask the members to individually post their answers. Discuss the variations and come to a consensus on what business the team is in.
- Prior to a teleconference, assign team members to work in pairs via e-mail, phone, etc., to create a statement that describes the business they are in. Have each pair post its answer on a team blog or Web site. Discuss and come to agreement on a definition during the teleconference.

Importantly, business is best defined *not by what a company or team sells, but by what its customers want to buy*. There is a difference.

Companies that saw themselves as being in the music CD business, for example, were generally unable to survive when their customers started downloading music. Companies that saw themselves as being in the music business, however, were more likely to embrace the newer technologies and find a way to make money with them. This pattern has repeated itself over and over, in industry after industry.

Consider another example: People who see themselves as selling insurance will tend to act one way. People in the same industry, however, who see themselves as selling security (or peace of mind) will use a whole different approach. Guess who sells more insurance?

Basic Economics

Most companies are in business to make a profit. The number of compa-

TRICKS OF THE TRADE

STIMULATING DISCUSSION

To have an interesting basic business discussion with your virtual team, have the members answer the following questions:

1. What products/services does our team provide? (By the way, if there isn't an answer to this first question, your team members wouldn't be receiving a paycheck. Never settle for an answer like "We don't really provide a product or service for anyone.")
2. Who are our customers? (The answer shouldn't be "senior management." Think of your management as your banker, not your customer. Of course you have to be responsive to management, or your "funding" might be cut off. But management needs are usually different from customer needs. Push the discussion until you get to the people who pay money for a product or service.)
3. What customer needs do these products and services meet?
4. How else could customers meet these same needs?
5. What are some shifts in the marketplace that could cause us to change our products or services to stay in business? What kinds of changes would we have to make in our team to accommodate those modifications to our products or services?
6. If done properly, by the end of this conversation you should see people thinking more like businesspeople than employees or hired hands.

nies that fail each year, however, is testament to the fact that this is more difficult than it appears. We can understand these business challenges better by reviewing some of the basic laws of economics.

WHY DO VIRTUAL TEAMS NEED TO UNDERSTAND ECONOMICS?

SMART

MANAGING

At a basic level, all team members know the importance of making money. But when asked to operate more autonomously, they need a deeper understanding of how basic economic concepts affect them. For instance, we often hear remote team members or those working third shift complain that their manager doesn't accept their improvement ideas. In reality, the manager most often believes the idea to be a good one, but finds that it cannot be implemented because of economic constraints.

Such business realities may be somewhat clearer to collocated team members who are exposed to the daily scuttlebutt regarding business pressures, but may be unrecognized by those who aren't collocated. Hence the need to provide virtual teams with the fundamentals of business economics and how to use that knowledge in day-to-day work.

Simply put, for a company to be successful, it must produce the highest-quality products at the lowest-possible cost. Why? Part of the reason is that customers don't want to pay any more than they have to pay to get the product or service they desire. And they will pay less for what they perceive as lower quality and more for what they perceive as higher quality. This is called *value*. It is so predictable and consistent that it can be stated as a mathematical equation as follows: *Value equals the perceived quality of the product or service divided by the price.* Thus the higher the quality and the lower the price, the better (higher) the customer value.

| **Value** Perceived quality for the money. Products or services that are offered to **KEY TERM** customers as the highest quality for the lowest price are seen as high value. But quality is determined by the customer, not the provider. A product or service may be very inexpensive to produce or provide but still be perceived by customers as high quality. Conversely, a product or service may be very expensive to produce or provide but still be perceived by customers as low quality. |

Prices are determined not by what it costs to produce a product but by "what the market will bear" (what customers will pay). If a company can't produce its product or service for less than the price a customer will pay, the company goes out of business.

Another thing required to be successful in business is meeting shareholder expectations. Shareholders are the people who own shares in your company. Unlike customers, shareholders are very predictable. They always want the highest possible return from their investment. Period. Unsatisfactory shareholder returns can cause tremendous pressure on the company to make improvements in its profitability.

Understanding Customer Expectations

One important and effective way to focus virtual team members on the larger business picture rather than on just their piece of the puzzle is to keep them connected with customers. This begins by making sure all team members have a clear understanding of customer expectations. This is most effectively accomplished when members themselves gather customer information and track it over the life of the product or project.

TRAINING VIRTUAL TEAM MEMBERS
ABOUT BASIC ECONOMICS

SMART

MANAGING

A good way to train your team about basic economics is to have the members consider their own experience as a customer by asking questions such as:

1. Think of a recent personal shopping experience. Did you buy the most expensive, more moderately priced, or least expensive item? Why?
2. As a customer, what do you expect of the products or services you purchase?

Then have them think about the customers of their team's products and services with questions such as:

3. What affects the value of our products/services (as seen from the perspective of our customers)?
4. What affects the perceived quality of our products/services?
5. What could we do to increase the value of our products/services?
6. Would you describe your business situation as not very competitive, competitive, or very competitive? How does that affect the price we can charge our customers?

Virtual teams need to first understand that the single best strategy for business success is to give customers what they want, at a price they are willing to pay, when and how they want it. All virtual team members must understand these critical requirements.

Here are some tips for obtaining information from the customer:

Start with what you have. Most organizations that have managed to survive know a lot about their customers. If you don't already know who your customers are and what they want from you, find out who does know. Chances are there are people in the organization, such as sales and marketing specialists, who have this information. Speak with them.

If possible, get firsthand information from your customers. Nothing substitutes for getting customer information directly from the customer. Many companies arrange to have customers visit with team members during virtual meetings. Others send out employees to gather data from customers.

There are some simple guidelines that can greatly enhance your team's ability to interact with customers and gain insightful information regarding their expectations.

SMART

MANAGING

THE VOICE OF THE CUSTOMER

Few interactions are more powerful for virtual team members than a contact with actual customers of their products or services. Arranging for this can be tricky because you don't want to risk offending or losing a valued customer, but if you can pull it off (usually by careful coordination with your salespeople), a conference call with a customer during a virtual team meeting can drive home important points such as:

- Why deadlines are so important
- Why you can't let quality slip
- What customers see as the most important things in your product or service
- Why you have to be concerned about cost
- Why you have to stay ahead of the competition

This information is so much more powerful if it comes from the customer instead of management. And it can serve as a reminder of how to work when managers aren't there to direct virtual team members.

Pair up when possible. When discussing expectations with a customer, it is helpful to do it with another team member. Doing so enables team members to gather more information and insight from the interaction. It will also show the customer that you are serious and consider what the customer has to say as important. This is tricky when team members are spread across time, space, and culture. Consider options such as a well-prepared teleconference interview with a customer where two team members can participate. Or look for opportunities to have customers join the team for an hour or two when the team is meeting face-to-face.

Ask good questions. Customers have a tremendous amount of information to share. The purpose of interviewing them is to gain access to that information. The best tools for gathering that information are the questions you ask. In most cases, it is helpful to ask questions that cannot be answered by a simple yes-or-no response. For example, ask, "What do you expect in terms of response time by our team?" instead of "Do you expect our team to provide fast response time?"

Get to the specifics. Often customers will describe what they want in very abstract terms. They might use expressions like "fast response," "high quality," or "courteous treatment." It is important to develop an understanding of what these terms mean to the customer. It may be useful, for example, to establish upper and lower limits of what is acceptable. The more specific the information gained from the customer, the more useful it becomes when making decisions and dealing with customer issues.

Listen, listen, and listen. Customers know what they want better than you do, so listen carefully to what they have to say. Remind team members that the goal is to find out what the customer expects. A good rule of thumb is to let the customer do about 80 percent of the talking. The team members' 20 percent should consist primarily of asking questions and clarifying important points.

Avoid getting defensive. It is possible that customers will give you some negative feedback. A natural reaction is to get defensive and make excuses. Coach virtual team members to avoid this. It may be especially difficult when interviews are done virtually rather than face-to-face. Remind team members that the team needs to know how the customer really feels. Feedback about what has gone wrong in the past can be valuable. If the interviewer feels an explanation is necessary, it should be provided in a way that shows an understanding of the problem and a desire on the part of the team to make things right.

Summarize what you heard. There is no better way to check for understanding than to summarize what you heard the customer say. When summarizing, attempt to use some of the customer's expressions and descriptions to show your understanding. Emphasize key points. After the summary, ask the customer for feedback: "How did I do?" or "What would you add?"

Do not overcommit. One big temptation when clarifying expectations with customers is to make promises that your team cannot deliver. Remember the old axiom, "It is far better to underpromise and overdeliver." If promises are made to customers to make them feel better about your team, but then your team cannot follow through, it will erode customers' confidence and trust in the team. It is better to commit to what is reasonable and then work hard as a team to exceed what you committed to.

Working with Business Partners

Most virtual teams have products and services integrated with those of other teams to provide an end product to the final customer. Your team, for example, might provide the service of creating new product designs that have to be produced and sold by other teams, or perhaps your team ensures compliance to regulatory standards established for procedures performed by your partners in various labs. To help team members better understand these processes and relationships, consider Figure 10-1, which shows a diagram of what business experts call the "open systems" model.

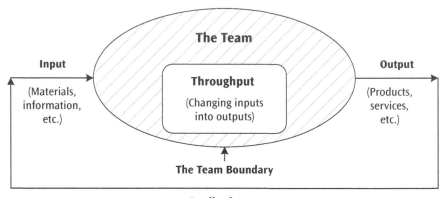

Feedback Loop
(Feedback from environment about outputs}

Adapted from *Leading Self-Directed Teams* by Kimball Fisher, used with permission.

Figure 10-1. The open systems model

As this diagram shows, any work process has "inputs" (information, raw materials, products/services from vendors, etc.) that are assembled during the "throughput" process into "outputs" (the products or services you sell to customers). For example, an information technology team might have inputs such as data from various financial interactions and software from vendors. The team's throughput is the data compiling and organizing process that results in the output of reports. Similarly, a factory may have inputs that include the raw materials used to create finished products and the production equipment used in the assembly process. The assembly process is the throughput. And the output would be the product.

Another important part of the open systems model is the environment in which your organization operates. Your environment would typically include a number of people who affect your organization such as customers, competitors, regulatory agencies, other teams, corporate headquarters, etc.

Large organizations often require that several teams work together to produce an end product. A virtual team of national salespeople, for example, may sell a product that is produced by several other teams in a series of steps such as mixing, packaging, and distribution. This is part of the "value chain." The value chain is the whole line of people from vendors to your team and your team's internal partners and on to your team's customers. For a business to be successful, each link of the value chain must be as strong as possible.

Value chain The collection of virtual partners who must work together to produce a complete product or service. If the service, for example, is helping patients in an emergency room, the external partners might include vendors like pharmaceutical companies, hospital supply stores, medical equipment corporations, laundry services, temporary worker agencies, and computer and software suppliers. Further down the chain, internal partner teams of nurses, doctors, administrators, clerks, technicians, custodians, security personnel, human resources, accountants, etc., within a hospital or group of hospitals coordinate together.

KEY TERM

Downstream external partners outside the hospital(s) such as laboratories, insurance companies, physician corporations, attorneys, police, medical transportation, payroll services, specialized diagnostic services, billing and collection agencies may also be involved. Improving a value chain normally requires special attention to the hand-offs and coordination between partners, even more than the improvement of the work processes within a given team.

For example, each group of internal partners (people inside the company) must work closely to ensure that the final customer gets the proper product or service. Sometimes these people are called internal vendors (if they hand off to you) or internal customers (if you hand off to them). This wording has become less popular recently, however, because it sometimes dilutes the importance of the external customer. For example, some organizations have had problems when a team worked hard to satisfy the demands of an internal customer, only to find that it had a negative impact on the external customer by adding unnecessary cost or reducing quality. For this reason, many organizations prefer the word "partner."

Improving the Value Chain

How can virtual team members improve their business? One of the best ways is to improve the value chain by beginning with the end in mind: First identify the customer needs, and then work backward through the value chain to ensure that the needs are met. We suggest the seven-step process for improving the value chain outlined here:

1. Identify key customers.
2. Clarify customer needs.
3. Identify internal partners.
4. Clarify expectations of and for internal partners.
5. Identify key external partners.
6. Clarify expectations of and for external partners.
7. Monitor and discuss performance regularly.

Let's discuss each step in turn.

Step 1: Identify Key Customers

Agree on how the team will determine key customers (Who spends the most money? Who buys the most products? Who is most important to your long-term future? etc.) and then identify your team's top few customers (generally about five to seven customers).

Step 2: Clarify Customer Needs

Identify a good process for pinpointing customer needs (Talk with sales and marketing people? Do some selective customer visits? Review existing reports on the topic? etc.). After the team members gather the information, have them list the key needs (three to five) for each customer.

Step 3: Identify Internal Partners

Identify the internal partners (inside the same organization) your team works with to get your products and services to your external customers.

Step 4: Clarify Expectations of and for Internal Partners

Agree on a process to get information from your team's internal partners about what they need from you to meet customer needs. Use this process to share your team's expectations of them, as well. You might do this in a virtual meeting with all internal partners at once, or you might choose to conference with representatives of each partner organization individually.

Step 5: Identify Key External Partners

List the team's key external partners (both suppliers—the top few vendors who sell you their products or services—and any other people the team must work with outside of your organization to deliver your product or service).

Step 6: Clarify Expectations of and for External Partners

Identify a process to clarify external partner requirements and share your expectations of them. Remember to relate these back to the customer needs identified earlier.

Key considerations include:

- What does our customer need?
- When does our customer need it?
- How does our customer use it?
- What else is important to our customer?

As the team members obtain specific and measurable information regarding what the customer require from them, they will be able to specify what is required of the external partners. To determine what will be expected of external partners, consider the following questions:

- What products or services do we need?
- What are the key requirements of each product or service?
- How can we measure the key requirements?

Step 7: Monitor and Discuss Performance Regularly

The final step in the process is to monitor performance. Once expectations have been identified along the value chain, they must be monitored to determine whether they are being accomplished. A clear and measurable monitoring process that involves all of the right people provides objective data for discussing results and future goals. Monitoring and measurement methods might include the following:

■ Keep tracking charts and post them on your Web site.

■ Observe supplier or partner operations.

■ Ask for feedback from customers and partners through periodic e-mail, teleconference, or some other method.

■ Hold Web conferences with customers and partners on a regular basis to discuss the level of performance.

SMART MANAGING

TIPS ON SHARING PARTNER EXPECTATIONS
Achieving mutual ownership of the expectations requires two-way discussion and a certain amount of flexibility by all parties. It also requires that you involve the right people when discussing expectations. The people you talk with should have the authority to make commitments for their entire group or company. The expectations should be attainable and agreed on by the team. There should be few surprises. Requirements should be real and not padded to cover for poor performance. It is critical that both parties be honest and ethical throughout the relationship. Remember to voice your wants and concerns, but also be sure to listen to the views of others.

Improving business processes can seem a little tedious, but a careful consideration of the steps listed above can result in bottom-line improvements for your virtual team. We know some teams, for example, that have reduced costs by helping vendors eliminate unnecessary steps that the vendor assumed were required by the virtual team.

In one extreme and humorous case, for example, a team at Tektronix (Tek) had required of an Asian vendor that no more than 3 percent of the components provided by the vendor were allowed to be outside the quality parameters. Confused that Tek allowed *any* bad product, the vendor began sending a small box with each shipment that contained the 3 percent bad parts. When the Tek team confirmed that it would prefer no bad product at all, the vendor happily agreed, discarded the bad product (rather than shipping it in a convenient package to the customer), and offered a small additional discount to compensate for its reduced workload.

Manager's Checklist for Chapter 10

☑ Using a process to identify the key participants in your value chain can help your team streamline and improve its business.

☑ The key steps in the value chain analysis include:

Step 1: Identify key customers.

Step 2: Clarify customer needs.

Step 3: Identify internal partners.

Step 4: Clarify expectations of and for internal partners.

Step 5: Identify key external partners.

Step 6: Clarify expectations of and for external partners.

Step 7: Monitor and discuss performance regularly.

☑ The open systems model illustrates how each virtual team has three basic functions: input, throughput, and output. Each function is affected by the business environment. To improve our teams, we have to understand our business environment, including our customers, competitors, and regulatory agencies, etc.

☑ One of the most critical things virtual team members must understand (to have a high business IQ) is their key customers' expectations. Where possible, direct interaction with the customer is a powerful way to gather the data.

☑ Understanding basic economics, including the concept of value (customer-perceived quality divided by price), is essential for virtual teams.

☑ For teams to be successful, they must know what business they are in. The answer to this question is often more difficult to get right than it appears.

Note

Much of this information is from a workbook entitled *Business Basics* (The Fisher Group, Inc., 2010) that we use to train clients. Used by permission of the authors and copyright holders.

Teaching Finance Fundamentals to Virtual Teams

A business that makes nothing but money is a poor business.
—Henry Ford

ompanies are in business for more reasons than making money. But it is a naive virtual team manager who ignores the importance of profitability. Even though virtual team members are often more highly educated than their collocated counterparts, the methods for tracking profit and determining how to make good business investment decisions are often like a foreign language to them. A basic understanding of a few key financial concepts can serve as another substitution for hierarchy (in addition to the business basics discussed in the last chapter).

For example, when virtual team members understand their team budget, the information serves as a tool to help bridge the distance between them and reinforce their common goals (while also helping them to be more self-organizing). Collocated team members often get this information as a function of their proximity to a corporate office, where financial reviews in some form or another are a regular part of meetings and where they are often copied on a plethora of reports normally unavailable to people who are remote from offices.

We know few virtual team members who bemoan the fact that they miss these kinds of discussions and reports, which at first glance can seem to be little more than a distraction to their functional work or projects. But what they don't understand is that if they are in a for-profit enterprise, finance is the glue that holds the organization together. It creates a framework for thinking about the prioritization of work, the allocation of resources, and the monitoring of progress. Perhaps most importantly, without a basic understanding of finance, your virtual team members are disadvantaged when it comes time to consider people for promotion. You don't want them to be overlooked for these opportunities in the future.

In this chapter, we help you understand some of the most critical elements of reporting and managing company finances. We review budgeting and cost/benefit analyses and discuss how profit is calculated and how to read an income statement. Teaching this language of business to virtual team members will not make them financial experts, but it will help them be more effective business partners and help them overcome feelings of isolation. Unlike previous chapters, this chapter is a little more like a tool kit. We include some activities and resources you may find helpful to use in team meetings or training sessions on this topic. The last part of the chapter is a glossary of financial terms to use as a reference so your team better understands the foreign language of finance.

Budgets

Budgeting is a critical business activity that all virtual team members should understand. Businesses can't be successful without this method of projecting and managing the costs of doing business. But budgets— and for that matter, most financial reports—can be confusing because they don't use common words. Finding a way to help virtual team members understand their budget and how the budget affects their activities as a team can be a powerful way to inject more discipline into team discussions about money, resources, and financial accountability.

Calculating a Cost/Benefit Analysis

Another practical financial tool for virtual team members to understand and use is a cost/benefit analysis. Businesses must determine how to allocate their limited resources as effectively as possible. A certain

---

AN ACTIVITY TO UNDERSTAND BUDGETS

To help team members understand their budget, consider using the following activity in an upcoming Web conference:

Comparing Business and Household Budgets

TOOLS

Look at your team's budget. Write the various parts of the budget down on the left side of the whiteboard on your Web conference platform. Then, discuss how these apply to common household expenses. For example, the word "freight" in your budget might be like postage stamps used to mail letters, "utility expenses" might be like your electric and gas bill, and "salaries" might be like the money you pay for day care. Write these home examples down on the right side of the whiteboard and then send team members a copy after the meeting. They'll remember the discussion more using this method than if you simply send them an explanatory e-mail. Participation in a discussion always increases interest and retention.

---

amount of money is required to maintain the equipment and activities you already have, so companies have to be careful when deciding what new investments they should make. How do they do that? They look at which expenditures will yield the best returns.

To complete a simple cost/benefit analysis, divide the projected return (things such as cost savings, quality improvements, productivity improvements) by the cost

Cost/benefit analysis A simple mathematical analysis that helps you determine which options are **KEY TERM** better business investments. The bigger the benefit and lower the cost, the better the return.

required to get the return. Bigger numbers mean that you can get a larger return for a smaller investment.

This is a simple but powerful financial tool. When virtual team members express concern about company investments, it's a good tool to use to explain the practical realities about why one project is selected over another one. And this tool is a powerful way to empower people to make business improvement suggestions. When people think that something should be done differently, or that new computers or other equipment should be purchased, have them complete an analysis to see if the expenditure is a wise decision or not. Soon they will be eliminating certain sug-

USING COST/BENEFIT ANALYSES

CAUTION   Experienced virtual team managers understand that a cost/benefit analysis is less of a mathematical exercise than a logical one. When comparing various analyses to determine how to best spend company money, question the assumptions behind the numbers. An analysis that appears to be an excellent investment may be worthless if the projected returns are exaggerated. Conversely, what appears to be only a modest return may be under-estimating benefits. This is a key learning to teach your team.

gestions before they even bring them to your attention (because they don't make business sense to pursue), or even better, they will identify projects that offer significant cost savings or performance-improving potential that you will want to consider.

Hurdle Rates

Some companies have what is called a "hurdle rate." If you could do better on your investment by putting your money into a bank CD, for example, you would be foolish to invest those same funds into something as risky as a business investment. You have to do better than you could do in a low-risk investment to justify any business expenditure—this is the hurdle rate, or in other words, the minimum amount required to justify spending company money.

Payout Period

Some companies are interested in the length of time it takes to get the payout from an investment. An investment, for example, that pays out in one or two years (the entire investment has been cost-justified and you begin getting the return) is more desirable than an investment that takes four or five years to pay out. To figure the payout, determine how much the savings would be per year and then count the number of years until the savings pay for the original investment. For example, if a computer costs $1,000 and generates $500 in savings per year, the payout is two years ($500 first-year savings plus $500 in second year-savings equals $1,000, the original investment to buy the computer).

Understanding Profit

To understand profit, we first need to understand that there are different kinds of profit. "Gross profit," for example, is the profit that comes from taking the cost of producing goods and services (accountants call this the "cost of goods sold," or COGS) away from the net revenue (the sales to customers minus any returns, discounts, etc.).

But gross profit isn't the bottom line because it doesn't account for things like maintenance expenses, marketing expenses, or administrative expenses the company has to pay to stay in business. It also doesn't account for something called "depreciation." When a company has to buy major assets like buildings or equipment, most taxing agencies won't let the company deduct the total cost it paid for these assets all at once. It normally must distribute the costs over the lifetime of the asset. If a building has a useful life of 40 years, for example, the company claims a certain percentage of the value of the building over each of the 40 years. When all these operating expenses are taken away from the gross profit, you have what is called the "operating profit."

The bottom line is called "net profit" or "net profit margin." Net profit is calculated by taking the income tax the company has to pay away from the operating profit. This is the profit we are most concerned about in this chapter, because it is the true profit left over after all expenses (except shareholder returns) have been deducted.

Reading Income Statements

Most team members understand that net profit is what is left over when all expenses are deducted from all sales, but few understand how big the expenses really are. Every dollar paid by the company must be accounted for. This includes expenses to develop, produce, and sell the product such as equipment, facilities, energy costs, raw materials, and salaries. This information is found on your income statement (sometimes also called an "earnings statement" or a "profit and loss statement"). A sample income statement is shown in Figure 11-1 on page 135. These statements normally follow a basic pattern as shown in the figure.

Financial Terms and Concepts

We include a glossary of common financial terms below. Consider sharing something similar to this with virtual team members so that they have a sort of dictionary to use to better understand the language of finance. A

UNDERSTANDING PROFIT

Use the following activity to help your team members understand profit:

Select a time period for which you have good financial data (it may be last month, last quarter, or last year) and fill in the number of cents paid out of an average $1 of revenue for each of the expense items. The way to figure out the results is to get the percentages for the listed expenses. For example, if 20 percent of revenues is paid to taxes, you would write 0.20 in the blank across from taxes. If good data are not available, ask someone in accounting to make a best guess. Spaces have been left at the end of the list to remind you to include additional expenses unique to your organization.

TOOLS

Profit from an average dollar of revenue

SALES	$1.00
Materials	_____
Salaries	_____
Benefits	_____
Utilities	_____
Facilities	_____
Equipment depreciation	_____
Marketing/sales	_____
Maintenance/repair	_____
Rework/waste	_____
Taxes	_____
_____(Other)	_____
_____(Other)	_____
	_____ = Net profit or loss (Subtract all expenses)

After you fill out the form (you may want to do this with someone from finance on your teleconference or Web conference), ask the members of your team if they find any of this information surprising. Are any of the expenses different from they expected? Were they aware of how expensive taxes or benefits were? Did they know that all of these expenses had to be paid? If you have a virtual team with members on multiple shifts in the same location, having a finance person discuss this during a shift overlap meeting is a good idea.

collocated team member will often have more opportunities than your people will to attend meetings and ask questions about these topics. So a guide like this can be a lifesaver when a vice president copies them on an e-mail about the state of the business, or a senior manager asks them to

Net Sales	$100,000
Cost of Goods Sold	−$60,000
Gross Profit	$40,000
Selling and administrative expenses Depreciation and amortization Repairs and maintenance	−$20,000 −$2,000 −$2,000
Operating Profit	$16,000
Other income/expense Interest earned Interest paid	 +$500 −$1,000
Earnings Before Taxes	$15,500
Income Taxes	−$5,000
Net Profit (the bottom line)	$10,000

Figure 11-1. Sample income statement

respond to some questions about the financial aspects of their projects. Remember to double-check your terms with a trusted company financial expert before you publish a list. Some organizations use the terms below differently from the common usage, or they have company-specific terms you should substitute for the generic terminology.

Common Financial Terms

Accounting A system that provides information about the finances of a business.

Accounting period A period of time over which financial information is gathered.

Accounts payable The amount owed to a supplier.

Accounts receivable The amount owed to the company from customers and others.

Accrual basis Accounting for revenues in the period they are earned and for expenses in the period they are incurred.

Amortize or amortization The process for writing off intangible assets (such as copyrights, insurance coverage, and goodwill) over time.

Analysis A study or consideration of a proposed action.

Asset Anything owned that has value.

Bad debt An account receivable that can never be collected.

Balance sheet A financial statement that reports the assets, liabilities, and equity of a company at a point in time.

Bottom line Net profit or loss.

Budget Estimates of revenues and expenses for a particular period.

Capital Money and other property of a corporation. Can also refer to factories and equipment.

Capital expenditure An improvement (unlike a repair) that will have a life for more than one year.

Cash flow Anything that affects the flow of cash coming into and out of the organizations during an accounting period. You could, for example, look good on paper (have money in accounts receivable) without having the actual cash available to pay immediate expenses.

Certificate of deposit (CD) Common low-risk, low-return bank investment.

Competitive analysis A comparison of how your company stacks up to its competitors.

Cost justification A way to determine whether an investment will provide sufficient returns.

Cost of goods sold (COGS) The cost of producing goods and services, including raw material, labor, overhead, etc.

Creditor A person of business to which you owe money.

Customer The buyer of a product or service.

Debt An obligation to pay for something purchased or for money borrowed.

Debtor Someone who has debt.

Depreciation A reasonable tax deduction for the use of business property over its useful life. In the straight-line method, for example, if a computer cost $5,000 and had a five-year life, it would be depreciated by $1,000 for five consecutive years.

Equity Ownership of an organization.

Expense Business costs that can be deducted immediately (without amortization or depreciation).

Financial statements Balance sheets, income statements, or statements of cash flow.

Finished goods Products that are completed and ready for the marketplace.

Fixed asset Tangible property, such as machinery or buildings, used to produce goods or services.

Gross profit The difference between sales and the direct cost of goods sold.

Hurdle rate The minimum level of return required to justify an expenditure.

Income statement A financial statement (earnings report, profit and loss statement, or operating statement) that gives the results of operations between two points of time.

Income tax Tax based on income.

Inventory The raw materials, work in process (WIP), supplies, and finished goods.

Investment The purchase of stocks, bonds, annuities, property, etc., to create income.

Investor The person who invests.

Liability The equity or claim of a creditor.

Loss The negative difference that comes from selling products and services for less than it costs to produce them.

Net profit The money earned after all expenses, including taxes, have been deducted.

Operating profit The difference between revenues and related costs before income taxes or certain other expenses.

Petty cash A small cash fund for immediate expenses.

Profit The positive difference that comes from selling products and services for more than it costs to produce them.

Profit and loss statement (P&L) An income statement focusing on profit and loss information.

Return Earnings on an investment.

Return on equity (ROE) Ratio determined by dividing the earnings before interest and taxes by the equity. It shows a return on equity investment.

Return on investment (ROI) Ratio usually determined by dividing operating profit by unpaid liabilities and money owed to shareholders. Shows a return on unpaid investments in the company.

Return on total assets (ROA) Ratio determined by dividing the net income by the total assets. It shows the return on assets.

Returns and allowances Customer returns, discounts, and special deals that reduce sales.

Revenue Amount earned from sales and other sources.

Shareholder Owner of one or more shares of stock in a company.

Tax Money assessed to support a government.

Understanding these terms can empower your virtual team members to make better financial decisions and to feel like they are part of the company team.

Manager's Checklist for Chapter 11

☑ Using a financial terms glossary can help virtual team members without a financial background better understand the language.

☑ To read a simple income statement, it's useful to understand the concepts of net sales *(total sales minus returns and allowances)*, cost of goods sold or COGS *(the cost to produce products/services)*, selling and administrative expenses *(sales, marketing, and administrative costs)*, depreciation and amortization *(costs for wearing down assets and paying off liabilities over time)*, and repairs and maintenance *(costs for fixing and maintaining assets)*.

☑ To understand profit, it is useful to know the differences between gross profit *(the difference between sales and the direct cost of goods sold)*, operating profit *(the difference between revenues and related costs before income taxes or certain other expenses)*, and net profit *(the money earned after all expenses, including taxes, have been deducted)*. In most cases, team members will need to know that net profit is the "bottom line," because it is what is left after almost all of the expenses (except shareholder equity distributions) have been deducted.

☑ All team members should know how to complete a simple cost/benefit analysis by dividing the benefit of a potential activity or purchase (projected return) by the cost (investment). This is more of a logical exercise than a mathematical one, but it provides an important financial discipline for virtual team members to consider when they seek to justify spending company money.

☑ Financial prudence demands that each team have (understand and use) a budget.

Note

Much of this information is from a workbook entitled *Finance Fundamentals* (The Fisher Group, Inc., 2010) that we use to train clients. Used by permission of the authors and copyright holders.

Improving Communication and Feedback Skills

I start with the premise that the function of leadership is to produce
more leaders, not more followers.

—Ralph Nader

Most people would agree that communication is an essential
element of virtual team effectiveness. At the same time, however, almost everyone sometimes finds it difficult to express a
point of view or to understand the views of others. Effective communication takes practice and discipline. Especially when it must occur over
long distances.

This chapter discusses the basic communication process and the
characteristics of open and closed communication and reviews some of
the skills and techniques associated with getting your message across, listening to understand others, and giving and receiving feedback.

The Communication Process

On the surface, communication seems like a simple process. But when
studied more closely, we see that it is, in fact, complicated. Each individual brings to the communication exchange his or her own expectations,
background, biases, ideas, fears, wishes, etc. The process is further complicated by "noise" in the system, which can be anything from actual
physical noise (Has someone ever mistakenly hit the "hold" button

instead of the "mute" during a team teleconference? Suddenly, elevator music comes on!) to interruptions, emotions, accents, etc.

For example, it is important to remember that just because you said something to one of your virtual team members doesn't mean that the team members heard it. While you are talking, he or she may have been thinking about something else or may have not understood what you said but were reticent to interrupt you to ask a question. This is especially problematic when communicating across cultural distances, even if all members share a common language. When someone from the U.S. says "pants," for example, someone from the U.K. is probably thinking "underwear" instead of slacks or jeans. And when the person from the U.K. discusses a "bonnet" with her American colleague, he may be thinking "hat" while she is thinking "the hood of an automobile." It is useful to remember Winston Churchill's observation that the U.K. and U.S. are two countries "separated by a common language."

To minimize these problems, we encourage virtual team managers to take additional steps when communicating important messages. Although it takes extra time and effort, communicating this way increases the likelihood of understanding.

Getting Your Message Across

Remember these basic tips when communicating important messages across distance:

1. State the purpose of your message.
2. Communicate your message using these three components:
   a. **Main point**—Describe your idea, opinion, observations, concerns, etc.
   b. **Feelings**—Describe how you feel about the situation (e.g.,"I feel frustrated, angry, confused," etc.).
   c. **Effect**—Explain what you feel the effect of the situation is (e.g., is it affecting goals, group cohesiveness, safety, your personal working relationships, etc.?).
3. Listen to the response of others:
   Listen intently.
   Ask questions—Questions help you clarify and understand the responses you receive from others.

4. Clear up any misunderstanding:
   a. **Restate your purpose**—Go back to Step 1 and use different words to describe the purpose for communicating.
   b. **Restate the message**—Use different words to make your point, describe your feelings, and explain the effect.
   c. **Add meaning**—Provide examples and experiences to enhance others' understanding of your message.

5. Summarize:
   a. **Review**—Go over what has been discussed, what agreements you made, etc.
   b. **Plan**—Initiate any action steps that are needed as a result of the discussion.
   c. **Follow up**—Set a time to talk or meet again, as needed.

Empathic Listening

Our experience indicates that communication in virtual teams can be significantly improved through a process we call "empathic listening." "Empathy" is defined as "the ability to share in another's emotions, thoughts, or feel-

> **COMMUNICATION TIPS** **SMART**
>
> Keep the following guidelines in mind for more powerful communication with others:
>
> **MANAGING**
>
> 1. Take ownership for what you say and what you feel. Instead of saying "The team is concerned," for example, say, "I'm concerned."
> 2. Take responsibility for making sure you are heard and understood.
> 3. Use terminology and examples that your audience understands.
> 4. If you are on camera, be aware of your body language and what it might be communicating.

ings." "Empathic listening" is, therefore, listening to fully understand both the content and the emotions associated with the other person's message. Demonstrating empathy (e.g., "I think I understand why you feel that way," or "If I were in your position, I'd probably feel the same") helps the other person feel heard *and* understood.

While empathic listening means you listen to understand and empathize, it doesn't mean you have to agree

> **Empathic listening** To listen in a way that demonstrates that you heard both the message and the emotional content of the message.
>
> **KEY TERM**

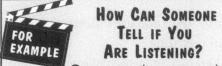

How Can Someone Tell if You Are Listening?
One way to demonstrate that you are really listening to others involves repeating what they said *to their satisfaction*. Once they agree that you have accurately heard them, you can move on to communicate your own points.

with the other person's position. It does, however, require that all parties avoid defensiveness in order to maintain a positive and productive tone in the conversation. If each person feels he or she can express forthright and honest opinions, the result is likely to be clearer understanding, better decisions, and improved relationships.

Empathic Listening Skills

Following are some of the key empathic listening skills. All these techniques feel awkward when you first employ them, but with practice they can become a natural and effective way to improve your communication with others:

Paraphrasing: Restating what you heard using different words. This is intended to verify meaning in ideas and opinions.

Examples:

I hear you saying that you're not happy with the procedure.

If I understand correctly, you would like to see us use a chart instead of a table of numbers.

Perception checking: Recognizing the feelings that you perceive in the other person.

Examples:

Susana, it seems that this has you upset.

Jan, I sense that you are nervous about conducting the meeting. Is that correct?

Inviting: Encouraging the other person to open up and tell you more. Indicating you're interested in knowing more.

Examples:

Tell me more about . . .

I'm wondering if you could explain . . .

Relating: Making the effort to feel what the other person feels.

Examples:

I imagine that it can be terrifying the first time through.

I can appreciate the frustration you must feel when you are dealing with a difficult customer.

Acknowledging: Demonstrating that you follow what they are saying and want them to continue.

Examples:

I see.

Uh huh.

Please continue.

Summarizing: Bringing closure to a conversation by reviewing main points, agreements, and action steps.

Examples:

Let me review what we have discussed …

Okay. I agree to let you know when I don't understand something and you agree to do the same for me. Correct?

BEHAVIORS THAT BLOCK EMPATHIC LISTENING

Here is a list of common behaviors that can block empathic listening in a virtual team setting. Try to avoid them!

- Thinking of what to say next while other people are talking
- Arguing about how others feel. Example: "You don't really feel that way!"
- Interrupting
- Assuming you know what others mean before they finish their message
- Prescribing solutions, giving advice, giving sermons
- Trivializing what others say. Acting as though it's not important
- Writing, checking e-mails or IMs, or multitasking while others are talking

---

Giving Feedback

An important characteristic of an effective virtual team is team members' ability and willingness to provide one another with feedback so that individual and team performance continually improve.

In traditional organizations, providing feedback is typically viewed as the responsibility of the supervisor or manager. In effective virtual teams, however, all team members see the feedback process as part of their responsibility. Team members are particularly qualified to participate in the feedback process for several reasons:

- Virtual teammates may know more about one another's work than the noncollocated supervisor or manager.
- Teammates know how mistakes, problems, or issues affect their own ability to perform the work.
- Teammates work on the process or issues regularly and may therefore have invaluable ideas for improvements.
- Providing feedback fits the values and principles of a high-performance organization.
- Sharing improvement ideas fosters continuous improvement.

Therefore, although this chapter is written for virtual team managers, the techniques discussed should also be taught to team members to improve the effectiveness of the feedback they give (and receive from) each other.

Purposes of Feedback

Too often when we hear the word "feedback" we think of correcting something that is inappropriate or unacceptable. While avoiding and eliminating errors is one purpose of feedback, it is just as important—if not more so—to provide positive feedback or feedback that builds on processes and behaviors that are already going well. Consider these three purposes of feedback:

1. *Feedback to reinforce, celebrate, recognize, or thank.* All of us appreciate knowing when we're performing well and that our efforts have been helpful in some way to others. Taking the time to acknowledge the positive contributions or good work of colleagues not only encourages good performance, but also helps build and maintain team morale. Sustained improvements are more often a result of positive feedback than negative.

2. *Feedback for continuous improvement.* These are situations in which things may be going well, but we have recognized an opportunity to improve even more.

3. *Feedback to correct.* Just as we need to know when we are doing things

well, each of us also needs to understand when we need to make a correction in our work or change a negative behavior.

The way in which you provide feedback is an important consideration. If the purpose of the feedback is to reinforce, celebrate, recognize, or thank, it is often appropriate to do so in public where other team members can share in the occasion. However, be sure to check with the individual first. While many people see public recognition of their efforts as a positive thing, some, because of personal preference or cultural differences, may find it embarrassing or offensive.

If the purpose of the feedback is to promote continuous improvement or to correct performance, it should be done in private. This protects the esteem of the individual and the confidentiality of the situation.

Practice Makes Perfect

Giving feedback is a difficult skill to master, but it does become easier with practice.

GIVING REINFORCEMENT FEEDBACK

Many virtual teams keep a "best practices" section on their Web page or wiki. This allows either you or other team members to acknowledge positive contributions and share them publicly with the team. You might post something like: "Mehran did a great job informing his vendors about the reorganization. I've attached the announcement he sent out so you can modify and use it to send out to your partners, as well." Or "Congratulations to Maria for completing her project on time and under budget (by 15%)!"

TIMING OF FEEDBACK SMART

As a rule, feedback is most effective when it is as immediate as possible. In some situations, especially if one or more of the people involved are angry, it is better to wait until emotions have settled. Another circumstance when immediate feedback may not be appropriate is when the person receiving the feedback is so preoccupied with other issues, problems, or projects that he or she will not have the time or energy to have an effective discussion.

MANAGING

Remember, feedback is intended to help the recipient more than the person giving it. Deliver feedback how, when, and where it will help the recipient— even if it may cause some personal inconvenience on your part.

Before sitting down to give feedback, consider practicing with a colleague or someone else who isn't close to the situation. Hearing yourself

WHEN SHOULD FEEDBACK BE GIVEN FACE-TO-FACE?

As we mentioned earlier in the book, certain types of performance feedback are best delivered face-to-face. Don't fire somebody, for example, through an e-mail or IM. Formal performance reviews are also best delivered face-to-face because the setting encourages open discussion, two-way conversations, and the best opportunity for clear understanding of expectations.

Realistically, however, virtual team leaders must be proficient at delivering feedback via technology. There are many types of feedback that can't wait for the next face-to-face meeting. Become proficient in delivering this urgent feedback by incorporating the tips included in this chapter. Some of the techniques may seem like overkill, but with practice you will see how including them improves your communication effectiveness where you don't have the benefit of a face-to-face venue.

talk helps you determine useful phrases or comments, and eliminate words or statements that may violate the principle of maintaining the self-esteem of others.

You won't go wrong even in a difficult situation if you remember that the only reason you give feedback is because you care deeply about the success of the team and of each team member.

SMART MANAGING

GIVING HELPFUL FEEDBACK

Feedback can be helpful or hurtful, depending on how it is delivered. Helpful feedback maintains the esteem of the other person, encourages him or her to recognize areas for improvement, and motivates that person to act on the feedback. Hurtful feedback creates feelings of distrust, resentment, and defensiveness.

Hurtful Feedback:
- The feedback attacks people and not issues or problems.
- The feedback is unrelated to the goals of the team.
- The feedback is given too late for the person to use it.
- The feedback is so sugarcoated that it has no meaning, or so brutally stated that the person can't hear it.
- The recipient is the last to hear the feedback.
- The recipient is not allowed to discuss the feedback.

Steps to Giving Helpful Feedback

The following steps can be useful when giving feedback. Depending on the situation, some of the steps may not be included. For instance, if the purpose of the feedback is to celebrate an accomplishment or a job well done, agreeing on future action may not be necessary.

State the purpose of the feedback. Relate the feedback to desired team results. This helps keep the discussion focused. "Mitch, I would like to talk to you about a concern I have. Do you have a minute now to talk?"

Describe your observations and perceptions. Be specific about the behaviors, incidents, facts, or perceptions on which you base your point of view. Be brief, but clear. Use cause-and-effect statements rather than accusatory statements when describing incidents or behaviors. Instead of saying, "You always turn your reports in late," it's more effective to say, "When you turn reports in late, it prevents us from completing our work on time," or "Over the last three weeks, the compliance reports have been turned in late four times. This prevents us from completing our work on time."

Listen to the other person's views. Having a joint discussion where all parties participate and share their thoughts is more likely to have a productive result. It helps both parties avoid defensiveness if they feel their views are heard and respected. Ask "is there a problem that's preventing you from getting the reports in on time?"

Jointly agree on action to be taken. Summarize the discussion. Offer to help in any way to improve the situation. Letting the other person know you are supportive will go a long way in reducing defensiveness. Be sure to summarize what you've agreed on before wrapping up the discussion. "How about if we work together to come up with a plan to help you get the reports in on time?" Or "OK, so we've agreed that I'll let you know ahead of time if the report deadline changes, and you'll let me know if you run into any problems that will affect your getting the reports to me on time."

Show appreciation. Receiving feedback is just as hard as giving it. Let the other person know you appreciate his or her willingness to discuss the issue or problem and to listen respectfully to your point of view. "Thanks, Mitch, for letting me talk with you about this. I feel better having discussed it with you. I appreciate your willingness to hear my feedback and work with me to fix the problem."

Guiding Principles to Giving Helpful Feedback

Realistically, you may find yourself in the middle of a feedback session before you've even had time to prepare. In such situations it is helpful to keep these guiding principles in mind:

- **Do not stockpile feedback.** Provide the feedback immediately after the situation occurs, unless you perceive that emotions are high.
- **Take personal ownership for the feedback you give.** Emphasize your feelings. Avoid generalities or speculation regarding how others feel.
- **Confront by focusing on the behavior or issue,** not the person.
- **Be sure to have a dialog with the other person,** rather than lecturing or dominating the discussion.

FEEDBACK PREPARATION WORKSHEET

Use these questions to prepare for actual feedback opportunities that you face.

TOOLS

1. How would you describe the feedback opportunity?
2. What is the purpose of the feedback (to celebrate or thank, to promote continuous improvement, or to correct)?
3. How does the opportunity relate to the desired results of the team?
4. What do I expect to change as a result of this feedback?
5. How urgent is the situation? Can it wait an hour, a day, or a week?
6. What are the facts, incidents, behaviors, and perceptions regarding the situation?
7. How receptive will the person be to the feedback, and what can I do to help?
8. Should the feedback be given in private or public? How should it be delivered? Is a face-to-face session necessary? If not, can it be delivered over a camera-less phone, or does it require cameras?
9. Who else, besides myself, should be present either face-to-face or virtually?
10. In what ways am I prepared to support and assist this person?

Receiving Feedback

Feedback is, of course, a two-way process. An effective virtual team leader or team member is good not only at giving feedback, but also at receiving it. And when you set a good example of receiving feedback from yor vitual team members, they will be more likely receive your feedback to them.

The following steps are helpful when receiving feedback:

Listen with the intent to clearly understand the feedback. Look at the discussion as an opportunity to gain information and insight. Allow the person to finish, instead of jumping in to defend your actions or behavior.

Ask clarifying questions or paraphrase. Seek to clarify the feedback you're receiving. Ask questions to clear up any confusion. Jointly discuss specific situations or examples that illustrate the points being addressed. Identify specific impacts on the other person, the team, and the business. Restate key points in your own words to make sure you understand.

Share your own views on the situation. Once you fully understand the feedback given, share how you feel. Provide information that may explain the behavior, while being careful not to make excuses or be defensive. Try to remain as objective as possible. Consider how you would view the situation from the other side of the conversation.

Jointly discuss and agree on possible ways to improve. Offer your ideas on how improvements can be made or the problem or issue can be resolved. Listen to the ideas of the other person. Make commitments regarding specific steps you'll take to ensure improvement. Express any needs you might have for assistance. Allow the other person to make appropriate commitments. Schedule a time to get together again and discuss how the action plan is working.

Express appreciation. Remember, it's easier for a person to keep quiet, avoid the risk, and not give any feedback at all. Giving feedback is not easy for most of us. Be sure to thank the person for helping you to recognize an important improvement opportunity.

There is a lot covered in this chapter. But if you can master the techniques reviewed here, your communication effectiveness will improve.

Manager's Checklist for Chapter 12

☑ Both the virtual team leader and team members benefit from improved communication skills.

☑ Both giving and receiving feedback are essential communication skills. It's important in any feedback situation to listen carefully, ask clarifying questions, offer assistance, develop an improvement plan, and express appreciation.

☑ It's a good idea to prepare for feedback sessions. It's especially important to be clear on the purpose of the feedback, to come prepared to give specific examples, to be prepared to explain how the behavior affects key business or team effectiveness indicators, determine whether it's best to deliver the feedback publicly or privately, and then to deliver the feedback in a timely manner, using techniques that allow for two-way communication.

☑ Avoid hurtful feedback. If it attacks people (instead of issues or problems), is delivered too late for the person to do anything about it, is too vague, or is unrelated to the goals of the team, it will hurt more than help.

☑ Feedback is not only for correcting performance; it's for continuous improvement and reinforcement, as well.

☑ Empathic listening is an especially important communication skill. Leaders who are skilled at listening to both the content and the emotion associated with a message are more effective communicators.

Note

Much of this information is from a workbook entitled *Feedback and Communication Skills* (The Fisher Group, Inc., 2010) that we use to train clients. Used by permission of the authors and copyright holders.

Chapter
13

Creative Problem Solving for Virtual Teams

If there is anything that a man can do well, I say let him do it. Give him a chance.

—Abraham Lincoln

The key to motivating virtual team members is empowered autonomy. But unless it is managed properly, a high degree of participation in decision-making and problem-solving activities by individuals spread all over space, time, and culture can be confusing, if not counterproductive. How does the virtual team manager provide appropriate coordination of these activities without inappropriate control? We discussed one critical method—boundary conditions—earlier in the book.

When a leader empowers team members to solve problems within certain parameters such as budgets, deadlines, and technology constraints, he or she is helping team members solve the problem themselves without micromanaging them to arrive at a specific answer. But in this chapter we review another important technique to supplement boundaries. When the leader of a virtual team controls the process instead of the person, the team member feels both appropriately assisted and empowered at the same time. In this way, autonomy is enhanced rather than diminished, and the probability of coordinated success is significantly more likely.

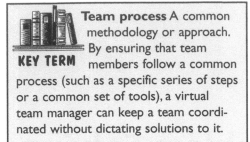

Team process A common methodology or approach. By ensuring that team

KEY TERM members follow a common process (such as a specific series of steps or a common set of tools), a virtual team manager can keep a team coordinated without dictating solutions to it.

How do you do that? By having a clear pathway or set of steps to follow to help your virtual team navigate the complexities and details associated with problem solving. The team members also need some practical tools to assist them. The basic problem-solving tools are the best for this, because they are easy to understand and use (with some practice).

This chapter introduces a simple six-step process for problem solving, along with a basic set of problem-solving tools. We also discuss a few advanced creativity tools. If the basic problem-solving tools don't work, use the creativity tools to get the team the team out of a problem-solving rut or help the team take a different, more creative approach to examining issues and solving problems. Here's a list of the six steps:

1. Define the problem.
2. Define success criteria.
3. Determine root causes.
   a. Determine where and when the problem occurs.
   b. Gather and study relevant information.
   c. Jointly agree on root causes.
4. Explore possible solutions.
5. Select a solution.
6. Implement the selected solution.
   a. Plan action steps.
   b. Take action.
   c. Evaluate progress.
   d. Celebrate.

Six-Step Problem-Solving Process

The following six-step process can be used to help a virtual team focus its problem-solving efforts.

Step 1: Define the Problem

Team problem solving begins by defining, as specifically as possible, the problem to be solved. The result of this step is a clear, concise problem statement. Having a well-defined statement helps assure that all team members understand the situation. It also provides focus during later steps in the process.

Sample Problem Statements. Below are a few examples of problem statements.

- Response time has decreased 30 percent over the last four months.
- Customer satisfaction ratings have declined 10 percent when compared with last year's customer satisfaction survey.
- Breakdowns on the Apex equipment have doubled over last quarter.
- Engineering is not meeting our three-week lead time for design specs.
- Morale survey results are significantly lower than they were last year.

WHY IS DEFINING THE PROBLEM SO IMPORTANT?   SMART

MANAGING

The temptation for many virtual teams is to skip directly to the solutions before the problem is clearly identified. This is because they are action oriented. But they might waste a lot of time downstream by refusing to invest a little time up front.

The members of one virtual team, for example, who were fed up with the glut of e-mail clogging their computers and wasting valuable storage space, were well under way in the process of finding a new e-mail provider before they discovered an important point. It wasn't the e-mail system itself that was the problem, but the way the system was used. Aborting their efforts to install a new system, they created e-mail protocols (as discussed in earlier chapters) and the problem went away. But literally hundreds of wasted hours of time that had been invested in searching for functionality could have been avoided if people would have realized up front that this was a social (people) rather than a technical (software) problem.

Step 2: Define Success Criteria

Success criteria describe how things should be if the solution is successful. Knowing what constitutes an acceptable outcome provides focus throughout the problem-solving process. Like most of the steps in this process, Step 2 sounds obvious. But many teams have wasted time when they got to the end of the problem-solving process only to realize that their upper management was looking for one thing (reduced cost, for example) while their technical partners were looking for another (quick problem resolution regardless of cost, for example). Knowing this up front might have allowed them to look for a solution that met all criteria, and instead of later finding out that the process must be started over.

SMART **SOLVING PROBLEMS VIRTUALLY**

MANAGING

A collocated team can complete the problem-solving steps listed in this chapter through a series of face-to-face team meetings. But a virtual team seldom has this luxury. Use the best-quality, virtual-meeting technology you can for problem-solving activities. A teleconference is fine for short meetings or one-way communication, but the problem-solving process benefits from telepresence approaches that allow everyone to view, for example, both a PowerPoint presentation of a problem statement (or list of root causes, etc.,) and the expressions of people who are watching the presentation.

When you see your engineering expert raise his eyebrows at one of the responses, you can say, "Bart, it looks like you're not sure about bullet number three," and draw out a better-quality discussion than you could over the phone. And don't assume that you have to be the one to facilitate the meeting. A problem-solving meeting is a good one to delegate to whoever has the best (or who most needs to develop) technical or problem-solving skills.

Step 3: Determine Root Causes

Often when describing a problem or issue, teams are more likely to identify certain symptoms related to the problem. Knowing what the symptoms are is important, but they do not tell the entire story. It is important to go further and determine root causes.

Root causes are the *reasons* behind the symptoms. For example, if you have a sore throat, you can easily locate the pain. That is the symptom. You can take cough drops and aspirin to treat the symptoms, but they will do little to eliminate the root cause. However, it may be more difficult to determine *why* you have a sore throat. It may be because you cheered too loudly at the game, or because you stood too long in the rain, or because you have a virus of some kind.

The result of Step 3 is a description of the underlying root causes associated with the problem. Those causes then become the focal point for exploring possible solutions.

MULTIPLE WHYS HELP YOU GET TO THE ROOT CAUSE

You usually have to ask "why" several times to get to a root cause. For example, the first answer to the question "Why is our communication less effective than we want it to be?" might be something like "We all need broadband connections." But answers to continued whys might dig deeper into answers like "Because our team-mates in rural India don't have the infrastructure for high-speed transmission." Why? "Because we choose technologies that are easier and more desirable for the U.S.-based team members." Why? "Because we tend to make technology decisions from a U.S. point of view." And why? "Because we are a U.S.-centric company."

Stopping at the first why would give you a different cause than stopping at the fifth why. In this example, you might spend a lot of money trying to fix a technical problem that ends up being only one symptom of a deeper cultural problem that requires a different type of intervention to solve.

Substeps for Defining Root Causes

a. **Determine where and when the problem occurs.** This allows you to target your analysis and avoid wasting time in areas that are not affected. By localizing the problem, for instance, you may find that it occurs only on one shift or only when using one communication technology.

b. **Gather and study relevant information.** Relevant information includes anything that can shed light on the problem under analysis. It can be obtained by observing a given process, keeping checklists, conducting virtual interviews, drawing diagrams, reviewing measurements and tests, creating flowcharts, reading reports, etc. Be sure the data are accurate so they don't lead you down a dead end.

c. **Jointly agree on root causes.** Using the information you gather, begin to form logical conclusions regarding possible root causes of the problem. Be certain that all team members agree on the conclusions reached, as this lays the groundwork for developing possible solutions.

Step 4: Explore Possible Solutions

Exploring various solutions enables the team to consider the problem from several angles, which usually results in higher-quality outcomes.

The solution process typically involves using brainstorming and

---

ROOT CAUSES VERSUS SYMPTOMS

FOR EXAMPLE Treating the symptoms makes you feel better, but it won't solve the problem. Conflict situations are a good example. Most often, conflict results from violated expectations, and is best resolved by clear and constant communication. This is more difficult to deal with over a distance. So when two members of the team are experiencing conflict, you might help them feel better by having them apologize to each other, but the root cause won't be addressed until you drill down far enough to understand the violated expectation. It is probably something like, "I thought you would do something you didn't do (take an assignment, follow through, ask for my input, tell me whether I sent you what you needed, etc.)," or "I didn't think you would do what you did (talk about me behind my back, throw away my work without asking, tell jokes about my accent, etc.)."

How do you fix that? Usually by helping people clearly identify what they expect when they work with each other ("Next time could you inform me before you make changes?" or "If you have a problem with me, let's talk before you discuss it with other members of the team," etc.).

---

idea generation techniques (discussed in detail later in the chapter). The outcome of Step 4 is a list of alternative solutions or approaches to the problem.

Step 5: Select a Solution

Having generated a list of alternative solutions, the team is now ready to decide which solution will be most effective at addressing the root causes. This usually requires a combination of *intuition* (what you feel) and objective *evaluation* (what your analysis tells you).

The end product for this step is a well-defined solution for addressing the problem. That solution can then be developed into an action plan with specific steps for implementing the solution.

Step 6: Implement the Selected Solution

The end product of this step is a solution to the stated problem.

Substeps for Implementing Solutions

a. **Plan action steps.** This includes determining *what* needs to be done, *who* will do it, *how* it will be accomplished, and by *when*.

b. **Take action.** Implement your plan. Remember to keep each other informed along the way.

c. **Evaluate progress.** Evaluation is an ongoing process that helps determine whether the root causes of the problem have been addressed, thus permanently eliminating the problem. Evaluating progress includes sharing lessons with others who might benefit from what you learned from the problem-solving process.

d. **Celebrate.** Remember to take time to celebrate a successful problem resolution!

SIMPLE ACTION PLANNING FORM

Here is a sample format that can be used to record your team's action plan.

WHAT	WHO	RESOURCES	WHEN	
Action	Person Responsible	Required Resources	Target Date	**TOOLS**

Consistently using a simple format like this can help a virtual team bring some order to its activities. The secret of managing virtual team problem solving is not the use of complex tools. Rather, it is the consistent and common application of simple, standardized ones that each team member can quickly understand, remember, and apply. You might post tools like these action plans on the team Web site at the end of each virtual meeting.

Many teams begin each meeting by reviewing the actions from the last meeting. They end each meeting by summarizing the actions coming from that meeting. This kind of discipline may not be essential in a collocated team, but in a virtual one, extra steps like this help ensure the clarity required by people who can't just pop over the cubicle and ask someone to try to remember who was responsible for a particular task.

Problem-Solving Tools

Broadly speaking, problem-solving tools can be divided into two major categories based on the kinds of issues they are most effective at addressing: (1) technical problems or (2) social or relationship problems. Many other books have reviewed the traditional technical problem-solving tools such as cause-and-effect diagrams, variance analyses, and Pareto analyses. But in this book we emphasize the tools for solving social problems that are especially useful for virtual teams. Specifically, we cover the Force Field Analysis, the Weighted Criteria Analysis, and the Start, Stop, Continue Exercise. Note that the Weighted Criteria Analysis can also be used for technical problem solving, as we illustrate below.

Force Field Analysis

The intent of a Force Field Analysis is to determine which forces are helping and which are hindering the team as it works toward some desired end. In reviewing the Force Field Analysis, it becomes clear that it is a composite of several other problem-solving and creativity tools. It involves brainstorming, cause-and-effect analysis, and weighted analysis. The end result is an informative, problem-solving tool that provides the whole-system approach necessary for high-performance work systems. The following is an example of how this tool could be utilized when facilitating a virtual team meeting:

1. Jointly agree on the desired ends. This should be a single, specific, and clearly written statement (e.g., "To develop a good working relationship with the salespeople" or "To get more resources for the expansion of the operation," etc.).

2. Divide the whiteboard on a Web conference meeting platform into two equal pieces by drawing a line down the middle of the whiteboard from top to bottom. Title the left half of the whiteboard "Helping" and the right half "Hindering." Brainstorm as a team all possible elements on each side. As Figure 13-1 shows, for example, if the problem is understaffing, a helping factor (things that would help improve the problem) might be extensive data that show your team is severely understaffed relative to similar virtual teams doing similar work. A hindering factor (things that make it difficult to solve the problem) might include a lack of understanding by senior management about your understaffing problem.

3. With the brainstorming session complete, the team should now weight the various factors. Obviously, there will be some driving and restraining forces that cannot be influenced (government regulations, technology constraints, etc.); however, those forces that can be influenced need to be rated by the team. The more important factors get longer arrows and the less important factors get shorter arrows. When completed, the diagram should suggest a course of action. In the example, a meeting between the team and senior management to discuss the understaffing data appears to be a possible solution that incorporates the most important variables on either side.

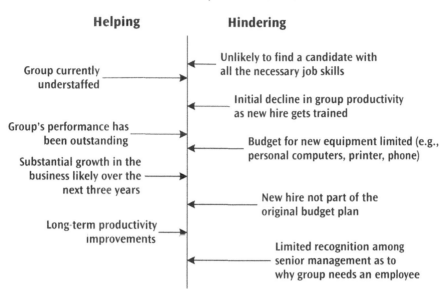

Desired end: To hire another person for our virtual team

Helping   **Hindering**

Group currently
understaffed

Group's performance has
been outstanding

Substantial growth in the
business likely over the
next three years

Long-term productivity
improvements

Unlikely to find a candidate with
all the necessary job skills

Initial decline in group productivity
as new hire gets trained

Budget for new equipment limited (e.g.,
personal computers, printer, phone)

New hire not part of the
original budget plan

Limited recognition among
senior management as to
why group needs an employee

Figure 13-1. Force Field Analysis

Weighted Criteria Analysis

The intent of this tool (the worksheet in Figure 13-2) is to help you make a decision considering multiple variables of differing importance. This is an ideal tool to use for virtual team hiring when some criteria, such as previous successful experience as a member of a virtual team, conversational fluency in English, or mastery of essential virtual collaboration technologies, may be more important than certain technical skills or educational accomplishments. To demonstrate the versatility of this tool, however, we explain how to use it to solve an operational rather than employee problem.

Using the worksheet involves the following steps:

1. **List and weight your criteria.** List one criterion in each of the spaces in the "Criteria" column. These criteria should describe the objectives you desire. Using a 10-point scale, assign a weight to each criterion to indicate its importance (1 = least important, 10 = most important). Record the corresponding weight in the spaces in the "Weight" colu,mm. As you can see in Figure 13-3, increased customer satisfaction was marked

Alternatives

Reducing Breakdowns		A	B	C	D	E
		Higher grade oil	Train employees	Buy new fleet	Preventive maintenance	Do nothing
Criteria	**Weight**					
1. Cost effectiveness	9	9 / 81	6 / 54	2 / 18	7 / 63	8 / 72
2. Stress reduction	5	4 / 20	3 / 15	9 / 45	6 / 30	2 / 10
3. Decreased overtime	6	5 / 30	4 / 24	8 / 48	7 / 42	2 / 12
4. Decreased crisis situations	7	5 / 35	6 / 42	7 / 49	9 / 63	2 / 14
5. Increased customer satisfaction	10	5 / 50	2 / 20	10 / 100	8 / 80	2 / 16
6. Long-term prevention	8	4 / 32	5 / 40	5 / 40	8 / 64	2 / 16
7. Management satisfaction	7	7 / 49	6 / 42	1 / 7	7 / 49	5 / 35
Total Score		**297**	**237**	**307**	**391**	**189**

Figure 13-2. Weighted criteria worksheet

by this team as a more important criterion (by two times) than stress reduction as it pertains to trying to reduce vehicle breakdowns.

2. **List your options.** List the options your team has identified in the "Alternatives" columns. These alternatives represent the choices available to your team.

3. **Assess each alternative against the weighted criteria.** Ask the question "How well does this alternative satisfy this criterion?" If it satisfies it completely, give it a 10. If it doesn't satisfy it at all, give it a 0. Otherwise, give a score between 1 and 9, depending on how well it satisfies the criterion. Place your score in the upper half of the appropriate box. Complete this process for each option against each criterion.

4. **Multiply each score against the criterion weight.** This gives you a weighted score. Place the weighted score in the lower half of each box.

5. **Add up the weighted scores for each alternative.** This gives you a total weighted score. The higher the score, the closer that option comes to meeting the success criteria you have identified. This worksheet provides you with objective data for making a decision. In the example, preventive maintenance is clearly a better solution than doing nothing or using higher grade oil. But remember, the decision is still the team's to make. Don't let the data decide for you. Use the data only as a tool to inform the decision.

Stop, Start, Continue Exercise

The intent of the Stop, Start, Continue Exercise is to improve working relationships among team members. This tool enables individuals to give and receive feedback on what they do that is helpful to others and what is not helpful, and receive ideas for how they can improve in the

---

VIRTUAL APPLICATION OF PROBLEM-SOLVING TOOLS

The tools in this chapter are common ones that have a long track record of success for team-based operations. In face-to-face meetings, they can be facilitated by someone standing at a chart stand, writing on a pad of chart paper. But if you use them **TOOLS** in a virtual meeting, you'll need to either use a Web conference whiteboard or purchase a groupware version of the tool for shared use on a network. Do a search on the Internet with the name of the tool to find the latest software applications and their functionality.

---

future. This tool can also help improve relationships with other teams or be a good way to begin a discussion about technology-use protocols (e.g., stop e-mailing me so much, start sending more IMs, and continue your quick response to my questions). One of the reasons this tool is so useful is that it requires people to share balanced (both good and bad) feedback. Feedback is much more likely to be heard and acted on when it isn't all negative.

The following steps are helpful when using the Stop, Start, Continue Exercise as a virtual team:

1. **Review the principles for giving and receiving feedback.** Being able to give and receive helpful feedback is an important part of the Stop, Start, Continue process. Before conducting the exercise, review the principles and techniques discussed in the earlier chapter on communication and feedback skills.

2. **Complete the Stop, Start, Continue diagrams.** See the example in Figure 13-3. Each person on the team writes a separate document for every other group member answering the following three questions:
   a. What does this person currently do that I would like to see stopped?
   b. What would I like this person to start doing in the future?
   c. What is this person currently doing that I would like to see continued?

3. **Share the Stop, Start, Continue documents.** Once the sheets are complete, they are shared with the person for whom they were filled out. In most cases the documents are collected and distributed by the virtual team leader.

4. **Develop action plans.** It is helpful to have all team members describe

Stop	Start	Continue
Sending me non-work-related e-mail (jokes and stories). Interrupting me during discussions.	Telling me openly and honestly when you disagree with me. Taking more credit for your ideas.	Your excellent technical work. Your honest, caring feedback. Involving me with you in solving problems that affect both of us.

Figure 13-3. Stop, Start, Continue diagram

what they feel about the feedback they received and what they plan to do as a result of it. To use the tool as a vehicle for solving problems between teams, complete the steps above as teams instead of as individuals. The Stop, Start, Continue tool can also be used to help a team as a whole review what it is doing well and where it would like to improve. In general, it is best used in instances where team mem-

> ### Sharing Written Feedback with Virtual Team Members
> CAUTION
>
> Subject any written feedback that will be distributed to virtual team members to the same scrutiny you would a performance appraisal document. Any poorly written feedback should be returned for repair, examples, or clarification. Peer feedback can be the most powerful type of feedback your team members ever receive, but if it is unskillfully delivered, it can be counterproductive, hurtful, or harmful.
>
> In a fully mature, high-performance work team, this kind of feedback should normally be delivered by each person who wrote it to each person about whom the feedback is written. But team members have to be well prepared and highly skilled to pull this off.

bers have full knowledge of each step of the process and voluntarily participate.

Creativity Tools

Sometimes the problem-solving tools described above aren't sufficient. Has your team ever been stuck on a problem that seems impossible to solve? Or have you ever felt the team was in a "thinking rut" and needed a boost to get its creative juices flowing? If so, you may need to use tools that help stimulate creativity.

Brainstorming

Brainstorming is a method for developing creative solutions by focusing on a problem and then coming up with as many solutions as possible. Every idea is recorded, no matter how bizarre, irrational, or unrelated it may seem when compared to the problem being discussed. Here is what's including the brainstorming process:

1. Define the problem.
2. Select who should attend the virtual meeting.
3. Review the brainstorming process.
    a. All ideas are valid.
    b. Build on each other.
    c. Do not evaluate yet!
4. Generate as many ideas as possible and write them all down in full view of everyone.

5. Clarify and eliminate duplication.
6. Evaluate list of ideas.
7. Have fun!

The strength of brainstorming is that it allows team members to feed off one another's ideas. Following are steps to ensure an effective brainstorming session.

1. **Define the problem.** All team members need to understand the problem to be solved.

2. **Select who should attend the virtual meeting.** Keep in mind the problem, people responsible for related tasks, and individuals outside the immediate team whose insights and perspectives may provide fresh ideas. Typically, the most effective sessions have five to ten participants.

3. **Review the brainstorming process.** Once attendees have gathered for the session, take a few minutes to review the "rules" of brainstorming:
   a. All ideas are valid regardless of how outlandish or unrelated they may seem.
   b. Feed off one another's ideas.
   c. Do not evaluate ideas until the end of the session. (Once individuals feel that their ideas are being judged, they will be less willing to contribute, thereby undermining the point of the brainstorming session.) Remember that even a crazy suggestion might trigger an excellent idea in someone else.

4. **Generate as many ideas as possible and write them down in clear view of all participants.** Seeing an idea is often what generates another one. Don't cover up ideas by erasing previous ideas on an electronic whiteboard to add new ones. All ideas must be visible during the entire brainstorming process.

   It is important that the scribe not reword or interpret what is said. This can discourage open responses or slow down idea generation. Comments are written exactly how they are said.

5. **Seek clarification and eliminate duplication.** Once the ideas are captured, it is time to ask questions and clarify the meaning of each one. This is also a good time to combine like ideas and remove redundant ones. Some teams will also schedule an incubation time to reflect on

existing ideas and to possibly generate additional ideas. This can be followed by a second brainstorming session.

6. **Evaluate the remaining ideas.** To reduce many ideas to the best few, some groups will use a process called "multivoting." For multivoting, each team member gets three to five votes to put on any item or items on the list. Members can use all their votes on one item or spread them across several. When votes are tallied, the list can be quickly narrowed to the top few items.

7. **Have fun!** Often a little lightheartedness is the best approach to creating an open and creative brainstorming atmosphere.

Brainstorming Variations

Below are a few techniques that can be used to vary the idea-generation phase of a brainstorming session:

- **One-at-a-time brainstorming** requires that each member speak in turn, offering one idea until everyone has had a chance to speak. This approach is often useful when certain team members are reluctant to jump in or when some team members tend to dominate. It is also helpful for certain cultures where people are reluctant to speak unless required.

- **Writing ideas down** is especially useful in situations where the atmosphere hinders open expression. Depending on the participants, it isn't always possible to create a sufficiently open atmosphere. This can be avoided by having participants write their ideas down rather than stating them aloud. This strategy can be especially helpful when people are not working in their primary language (writing gives them more time to think, whereas speaking requires immediate reaction). The ideas can then be texted, posted, or copied down by a facilita-

>
> **BRAINSTORMING TIPS**
> *Don't evaluate!* Even crazy ideas should be written down without comment.
>
> *Don't flip, scroll, cover, or erase!* Keep all ideas visible at all times.

tor. Still, all team members must be allowed to see all ideas.

- **Start the brainstorming session by reading a random word from the dictionary.** This can help "seed" the session, serving as a starting point for novel idea generation. Participants are asked to key off the initial word.

Creative Brainstorming

Creative brainstorming is a way of stimulating idea generation by changing one element in a problem definition (see Figure 13-4). The novel ideas, once generated, are then applied to the original idea. For example, session participants may want to brainstorm the issue of how to get team members comfortable talking to customers. According to creative brainstorming, the session participants would begin by creating an imaginary problem, such as how to help team members learn to use a computer.

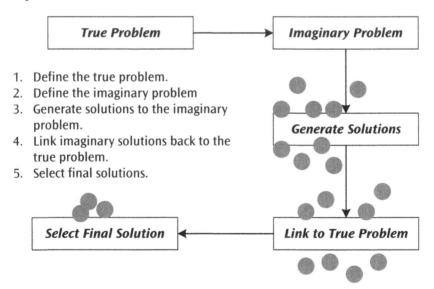

1. Define the true problem.
2. Define the imaginary problem
3. Generate solutions to the imaginary problem.
4. Link imaginary solutions back to the true problem.
5. Select final solutions.

Figure 13-4. Creative brainstorming

The ideas generated for the imaginary problem can then be applied to the real problem to see if any are applicable. We were working with one client, for example, who had a major employee retention problem. They tried everything they knew how to do to solve the problem with no success. When we introduced them to this tool and encouraged them to experiment with it, the imaginary problem they selected to solve was "How do we eliminate lost socks in the clothes washing process," and one of the solutions was "Tie the socks into pairs." Most of the other solutions to the imaginary problem were, of course, completely irrelevant to the real problem of employee retention. But when one of the managers saw the "Tie the socks together" solution, he suggested they institute a mentor program for new hires. Each new hire was thereafter "tied together" with a mentor, and the retention problem went away.

A variation of this approach is to assign a different problem to a portion of the session participants. Once the session begins, a variety of solutions will necessarily develop in response to each group's assumed problem, enabling participants to feed off one another's diverse ideas. The end will be more varied solutions.

Reverse Brainstorming

Reverse brainstorming involves listing ways to achieve a goal opposite the one actually desired. If, for example, a team was interested in improving relationships with its suppliers, it would begin the brainstorming session by asking, "How can we best *ruin* our relationship with key suppliers?" What is most interesting about this process is that the ideas generated by using this technique are very often (unintentionally) the ones currently in practice. The result is not only new and varied approaches to the problem at hand, but also new information about which of the team's current processes may need to be modified or eliminated.

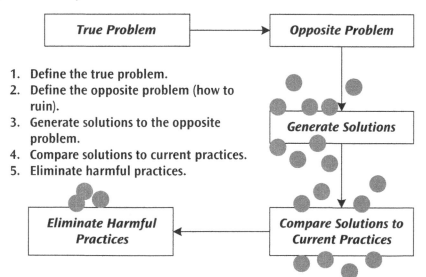

1. Define the true problem.
2. Define the opposite problem (how to ruin).
3. Generate solutions to the opposite problem.
4. Compare solutions to current practices.
5. Eliminate harmful practices.

Figure 13-5. Reverse brainstorming

Brainwriting

Brainwriting is a method of stimulating new ideas through sharing thoughts linearly. Whereas brainstorm participants are *allowed* to key off one another's responses, participants in a brainwriting session are *required* to do so. As Figure 13-6 shows, each person generates three possible solutions to the problem at hand. Each participant then sends his or her solutions to another person. The recipient writes down three additional ideas inspired by the ones already written and sends the list to another team member. The process is repeated until each recipient receives his or her original set of ideas. This is one tool that works just as well (or better) in a virtual as in a face-to-face setting. For the virtual application, use e-mail to start each list. Then have each person start a chain e-mail with his or her three points on the bottom, and the next person's response above that, and the next person's above that, and so on. The only requirement about the order in which the e-mails should be

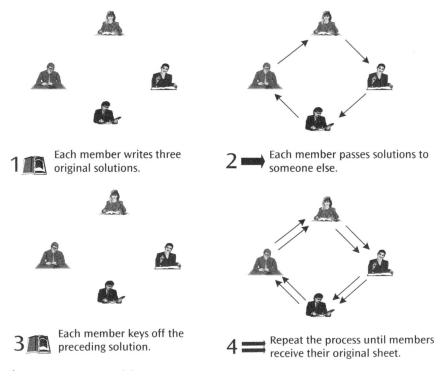

1 📖 Each member writes three original solutions.

2 ➡ Each member passes solutions to someone else.

3 📖 Each member keys off the preceding solution.

4 ⇉ Repeat the process until members receive their original sheet.

Figure 13-6. Brainwriting

sent is that the originator needs to be the last one to receive the final list. The e-mails can be completed prior to the virtual meeting, and then during the meeting the final lists can be shared.

Remember that these types of creativity and general problem-solving tools are like physical tools in many ways. Each tool is good for some situations and useless for others. Choose the right tool for the job. You wouldn't use a technical problem-solving tool, for example, to solve a people problem, anymore than you would choose a screwdriver to pound in a nail.

Manager's Checklist for Chapter 13

☑ An important way to maintain the empowerment of remote team members is to use a standard problem-solving process, with a handful of common problem-solving tools. This allows the team members to solve the problems themselves, coming up with solutions that are adapted to their situations and interests. But it still provides the consistency and coordination necessary for good results.

☑ A simple (and therefore repeatable) six-step problem-solving process is:
1. *Define the problem.* Sometimes the solution is obvious when the problem is clearly defined.
2. *Define success criteria.* How will you know when it's solved?
3. *Determine root causes.* What really causes the problem? How do you know?
4. *Explore possible solutions.* Look at several options for eliminating root causes before selecting something.
5. *Select a solution.* Have a good reason for your selection.
6. *Implement the selected solution.* Have and execute a plan. Follow up to ensure the problem was solved.

☑ Three dependable problem-solving tools that any good virtual team manager should have in his or her tool kit include:
1. *Force Field Analysis.* By identifying both helping and hindering factors you have a better chance to solve people-related problems.
2. *Weighted Criteria Analysis.* By forcing yourself to prioritize the importance of your criteria, you solve problems more efficiently and effectively.

3. *Stop, Start, Continue Exercise.* By organizing discussions into three common categories affecting behavior, you have a better chance of solving people-related problems.

✅ Four good creativity tools that a virtual team manager may need to teach people if the basic problem-solving tools fail (because the team is stuck and needs to look at things differently) include:

1. *Brainstorming.* If you follow the rules (no evaluations, write what people say, keep everything visible), you'll get more potential solutions of a higher quality than you would have had before brainstorming.

2. *Creative brainstorming.* By solving a completely unrelated problem, you see if any of the unrelated solutions might fit or be adapted to fit your situation.

3. *Reverse brainstorming.* By discussing how to make your problem worse, you determine if you are unintentionally sabotaging yourself.

4. *Brainwriting.* By forcing one another to look at previous responses and come up with three potential new solutions for every round of the activity, you see if you can find a few workable gems.

✅ Remember to use the right tool for the job. No single problem-solving tool can work for everything. Keep a number of them handy in your tool kit just in case.

Note

Much of this information is excerpted from a workbook entitled *Creative Problem Solving* (The Fisher Group, Inc., 2010) that we use to train clients. Used by permission of the authors and copyright holders.

Chapter 14

Managing Performance from a Distance

Never doubt that a small group of thoughtful, committed people can change the world. Indeed, it is the only thing that ever has.

—Margaret Meade

Almost any manager will tell you that performance management, under the best of conditions, is difficult. The very words "performance management" conjure up all kinds of negative images—disciplinary action, confrontation, and the dreaded annual performance evaluation process—to name just a few. For those managing remote employees, the process can seem even more daunting. But take heart. If you are managing remote employees, there are proven techniques to help you in managing team and individual performance.

In this chapter we first discuss some performance management basics, including clearly defining expectations, establishing a performance management routine, and regularly evaluating progress toward established goals. Later we address goal setting, accountability systems, and Individual Development Plans (IDPs) as tools for managing performance. We also introduce a technique called "Socratic coaching" that can be used to help those working remotely to improve performance.

Performance Management Basics

There are a few fundamentals of performance management that, when followed, help ensure the success of the team and each individual team member. These basics include establishing clear expectations and determining a performance management routine where goals can be discussed and feedback given. This requires regular virtual team meetings (typically teleconferences, video, or Web conferences), one-on-one phone calls, and occasional face-to-face team meetings.

SMART

MANAGING

THE IMPORTANCE OF FACE-TO-FACE MEETINGS

The term "virtual team" implies that these are teams or individuals that never come together physically. In reality, however, a clear majority of those who work in virtual settings strongly advocate having some face-to-face interaction. Times when face-to-face meetings may be appropriate or useful might include:

- *The team's kick-off meeting:* Having the opportunity to meet one another in person before launching into a day-to-day routine begins to build trust and rapport among team members. A face-to-face discussion of goals, roles and responsibilities, and boundaries helps the group coalesce.
- *Milestone reviews or celebrations:* Having periodic face-to-face meetings to review the status of projects or to celebrate accomplishments helps the team maintain momentum.
- *When the team needs to address issues that are particularly sensitive or clarity is needed:* Greater clarity and less misunderstanding may be achieved when the team is working on interpersonal issues or having discussions about critical project data in a face-to-face setting where maximum interaction (questions, debate, disagreement, etc.) is more likely.

Establishing Clear Expectations

Perhaps no other factor is more critical to a virtual team member's success than having clear expectations. When working from a remote location without the advantages of daily interactions with the team leader or other team members, a clear understanding of what each employee is expected to accomplish is critical to motivation and satisfactory performance.

Creating a Performance Management Routine

Each virtual team leader needs to establish a regular routine for reviewing and discussing performance, both with the team as a whole and with

SETTING EXPECTATIONS FOR REMOTE EMPLOYEES

When providing performance coaching and direction to virtual team members, consider these questions as a way to clarify expectations, each of which needs to be answered *to the satisfaction of the employee*:

- What am I supposed to do?
- How am I supposed to do it?
- How will I know when it has been done correctly?
- How do I get the resources (skills, tools, information, etc.) I need?
- How do I prioritize my activities?

each individual team member. Our research indicates that the recommended frequency is weekly teleconferences or Web conferences with the entire team. This enables the team to keep abreast of progress and helps you answer questions the team may have regarding its daily work or a particular project. Additionally, each team member needs to have the opportunity to "meet" with the team leader about every two weeks in a one-on-one setting. These conversations (usually teleconferences) allow you to provide regular performance feedback.

A third element of a strong performance management routine is face-to-face meetings (recommended quarterly or semi-annually). Face-to-face sessions facilitate team building and foster trust between team members and the leader. Discussing key organizational and performance issues in this setting allows the team to focus and go deeper into subjects than is typically possible in a virtual conference setting.

HOW OFTEN SHOULD A VIRTUAL TEAM MEET?

Our experience suggests a certain minimum frequency of interaction is necessary for virtual teams to be successful:

- Weekly team meetings (normally teleconferences, video conferences, and/or Web conferences)
- One-on-ones every two weeks (via technology)
- Face-to-face meetings quarterly or semi-annually

We have uncovered successful virtual teams that meet less regularly than these recommendations. We know, for example, of a few that have never met face-to-face. But these teams are the exception, not the rule, and their managers have to put in a lot of extra effort to avoid the predictable problems that come from teams that are starved for information and feedback. It is usually a serious mistake to skip these interactions.

Regular Evaluation of Progress

None of us can be successful without knowing how we are doing and having the opportunity to make adjustments when performance gets off track. Some leaders will build this discussion into their meeting agendas. For instance, one leader we know reviews goal progress every other week in her regularly scheduled team teleconferences. Another chooses to do it monthly during the first teleconference of the month. When and how often these updates occur are best decided jointly between the leader and the team. However, we recommend that some kind of formal evaluation be done at least monthly to keep the team focused and coordinated.

Goal Setting and Accountability Systems

Imagine being in a sports competition without knowing the rules, player positions, or the score. It would be frustrating, right? It is equally frustrating not to know the goals, accountabilities, or measures of a work team, especially when you aren't collocated or working during the same hours. Without knowing what you are supposed to accomplish, who has what responsibilities, and whether you are on track, teams working remotely can flounder, lose focus, and fail to achieve the highest levels of performance.

Consider the following case.

Mini-Case: Lars and the Disconnected Team Members

Lars is the leader of a remote team with members located in four countries and four time zones. He was asked to take this position three months ago when the former team leader retired. Eager for the opportunity to manage, Lars started out positive and excited about the team's potential. He learned rather quickly, however, that there were some serious issues facing this team. His first realization, for instance, was that the team's goals seemed random, and focused on a lot of activities related to each individual location rather than to the organization as a whole. There didn't seem to be any continuity across the team or interrelation of goals.

Second, none of the goals seemed related to the key organizational goals and objectives outlined by senior management at the beginning of the fiscal year. Lars was also concerned when he asked each location to e-mail him its current tracking charts. No one was tracking group progress. Richard and Christina in the New York office explained that they all just tracked their own goals. Lars is worried. The corporate leaders told him that when he took over, the team's performance for the last four years was less than optimal and that they hoped he could move the team forward. "How can I do that?" he wondered to himself. "These people don't have a clue what their performance is or how it is impacting the rest of the organization!"

Case Discussion

Many virtual team members move through their daily routines without understanding their connection to the larger entity or how they can impact the organization's performance. Some don't have clear goals and priorities, whereas others have so many goals that team members are confused and discouraged. Those that are most successful know how to set goals, establish team accountability for achieving those goals, and how to track and communicate them. For these virtual teams, being separated by space, time, or culture doesn't interfere with their ability to succeed.

Six-Step Goal-Setting Process

The following six-step process can help to meet this challenge and ensure the team's success:

1. **Define key result areas (KRAs):** KRAs identify the broad areas in which the team should focus its energies and provide a basis for measuring team accomplishments. Be sure to link your KRAs to what your customers expect of you and to integrate your KRAs with other partners inside your organization.

2. **Identify benchmarks:** "Benchmarking" is the practice of defining the best performance, and helps your team define meaningful standards. It also helps the team identify what is possible. When identifying benchmarks, first determine which employees are best, learn what they do, and determine how they measure what they do.

3. **Measure current performance:** In this step you determine the gap between the benchmarks you have researched and your team's current performance. The gap between where your team is currently

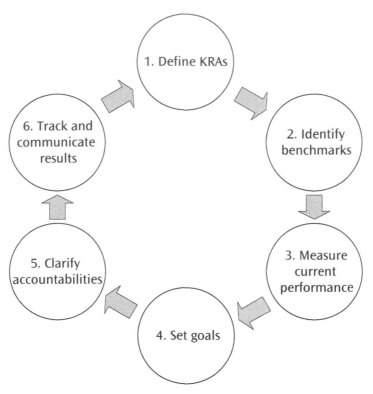

Figure 14-1. Six-step goal-setting process

performing and the benchmark becomes the focal point for setting team goals and establishing continuous improvement objectives. Common methods for collecting current performance information include doing surveys, utilizing existing quantitative information, or meeting with customers and suppliers.

4. **Set goals:** This is the step that helps the team move its performance toward the benchmark. In setting team goals, first look at the difference between where you are (current performance) and where you could be (the benchmark). Then determine what would be a realistic stretch from current performance.

5. **Clarify accountabilities:** The essential thing to decide in any accountability system is *who* is responsible for *what* by *when*. These accountabilities can be posted on the team Web site or shared drive with key project plans and timelines so that everyone is clear on one another's assignments. It is important to regularly update this information.

> ### GOAL-SETTING BASICS
>
> SMART
>
> MANAGING
>
> When setting goals, remember that they should:
>
> - Include a clear, meaningful measurement
> - Describe specific action to be taken
> - Be written down
> - Include a completion date or time frame
> - Be challenging but attainable
>
> The most common mistake teams make is setting too many goals. When effort is diffused across too many priorities, morale and productivity suffer. Spend most of your goal-setting time whittling the list of potentially helpful goals down to the *critical few* required for the team to excel.

6. **Track and communicate results:** Current and ongoing measurement is essential to the goal-setting process. A goal untracked is usually a goal unmet. A few keys to tracking team results include (1) keep the measurements simple to read and understand, (2) tie the measurements to the team's KRAs, (3) review the measurements regularly (e.g., once a month during a team teleconference), and (4) Make the measurements visible (e.g., post them on the team's Web site or shared drive).

> ### MODIFYING FOR VIRTUAL OR TEMPORARY TEAMS
> SMART
>
> MANAGING
>
> The six-step goal-setting process assumes that your team is a natural work group that will stay together for an extended time. If you have a virtual project team, however, or a temporary team that will not stay together long, you probably want to modify the process to shorten it. You may not, for example, do as extensive a job on benchmarking if the project will be completed in a few weeks.

Individual Development Plans

Once customer needs and market opportunities are understood and organizational strategies and goals are in place, the next step in creating a performance management system is developing individual development plans (IDPs).

Most corporations have a process to help people plan for obtaining the skills necessary to achieve the highest levels of performance. For some it may be something as simple as an informal agreement the employee has with his or her manager about classes the employee will take to stay up to date. For others it maybe a more detailed and formal process that assesses the organization's needs and then aligns those with the development needs and desires of the employee. One of the most common methods for planning and coordinating skill development is the IDP.

Elements to Include in IDPs

Most IDPs share some common elements:

- An overview of the company's skill development needs
- An assessment of current skills available in the organization
- An assessment and review of personal development desires and preferences

Typically, once these assessments are completed, skill development needs are prioritized and coordinated with the rest of the team. A plan is then assembled detailing how and when these skills will be developed. Plans may include a variety of methods such as classroom training, on-the-job training, mentoring, and project assignments.

The IDP Process

What should be included in an IDP process?

- Overview of company skill development needs
- Assessment of current skills
- Consideration of personal preferences
- Skill development needs prioritized and coordinated with the team
- Plan includes how and when skills will be developed (training, mentoring, project assignments, etc.)

Socratic Coaching

A key part of performance management from a distance is teaching virtual teams how to solve problems on their own. How do you do that? One way is by asking questions instead of giving answers. We call this Socratic coaching. Socrates was a great teacher who discovered that students learned more when they had to learn on their own without depending on their teacher for the answers. The questions are intended to initiate learning and to help others learn through self-discovery.

Allowing team members to build inner skull muscle tone is essential in teams whose success depends on their ability to acquire, apply, and transfer knowledge in an environment where they don't

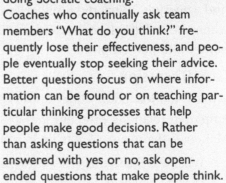

Socratic coaching A technique for developing employees by asking questions rather than by giving **KEY TERM** directions. It teaches individuals to think for themselves, instead of creating dependence on the remote leader.

always have immediate access to the team leader or other team members. To facilitate this development, coaches refrain from judgmental statements like "That won't work," instead asking questions like "What is the problem you want to solve?" or "How will you know when you have solved it?" or "What information did you base this conclusion on?"

If remote team members feel the only "right answer" is the one that comes from their manager, they will be unlikely to take action until they have, in effect, received permission to do so. Obviously, this can drastically slow down team progress when team members are in different time zones and have to wait a full day for a response from the manager.

By asking questions, the coach begins the process of transferring responsibility for addressing problems to team members. Questions also provide an avenue for helping team members think through the steps needed to come up with an effective solution. In this way, questions become a useful coaching tool. Socratic coaching is a skill that should not be undervalued when working across space, time, and culture. If done well, it teaches, strengthens, and empowers.

THE RIGHT AND WRONG QUESTIONS **CAUTION**
Be careful of asking the wrong questions when doing Socratic coaching. Coaches who continually ask team members "What do you think?" frequently lose their effectiveness, and people eventually stop seeking their advice. Better questions focus on where information can be found or on teaching particular thinking processes that help people make good decisions. Rather than asking questions that can be answered with yes or no, ask open-ended questions that make people think.

Consider the following case to understand how to apply Socratic coaching techniques.

Mini-Case: The Coaching Conundrum

Joshua is the leader of a team of eight HR representatives located at four sites in the same state. Five of the reps joined the company six months ago after completing their four-year degrees in Human Resource Management. The other three reps and Joshua are seasoned employees who have been with the company at least five years.

This is Joshua's first management position. He was promoted eight months ago just before the company decided to expand and and thus hire the new HR reps. There is no question that the first two months were easier than the last six. Working with the experienced team members was a breeze, and Joshua felt like things were well under control and in good shape. But once the new hires came on board, things definitely changed. They have so many questions, and it is difficult to get to each site often enough to feel he is teaching them all they need to learn.

Last week, for instance, McKenzie from the Westport office called six times with questions. They were all legitimate questions, but they were also things she had asked a couple of times before. For instance, she called once last month about an employee who had come to her to complain about his manager and wanted McKenzie to transfer him out of that group. Joshua had told her how to handle the situation and assumed she would be able to handle similar situations in the future. But then last week she called about an employee who said her manager wasn't promoting enough people in the group and she wanted McKenzie to help her find a new job. "What did I miss when I explained what to do last month when she called?" Joshua wonders. "This whole coaching thing is a lot harder with new employees!"

Case Discussion

What could Joshua do? Instead of explaining again how to address this employee relations problem, he could ask questions that would help McKenzie figure out what to do herself. Examples might include:

1. What was the manager's side of the story (instead of explaining to her that she needs to hear from everyone involved before making a recommendation)?
2. How have we handled these kinds of situations before (to reinforce the idea of respecting established precedent)?

3. What does the policy manual say about this (to ensure she has checked the policies before making a decision)?

4. What did you learn when you dealt with the earlier problem about a manager–employee disagreement? What could you apply from that case to this one (to remind her to keep building on her learnings)?

5. What alternatives are there besides transferring the employee out of the group (to get her thinking about other options)?

Manager's Checklist for Chapter 14

☑ Using Socratic coaching is a powerful way to develop people. When first employing this technique, you may want to prepare a list of questions that will get team members thinking about things like where to go to get resources and how to solve problems on their own.

☑ An Individual Development Plan (IDP) can be an important part of the performance management process. Each employee should know what skills the organization needs, and if the employee doesn't have them already, what he or she would have to do to develop the skills.

☑ Without goals, it is difficult for virtual teams to assess whether they are on track. A good six-step goal-setting process includes (1) define key result areas, (2) identify benchmarks, (3) measure current performance, (4) set goals, (5) clarify accountabilities, and (6) track and communicate results. If you skip any of these steps, your goals may not be challenging enough to make you successful in your marketplace.

☑ Clear expectations are necessary for people to perform. These expectations and your goals should be discussed in weekly virtual team meetings, one-on-ones every other week, and quarterly or semi-annual face-to-face meetings. Holding these meetings at these frequencies won't guarantee success, but it minimizes the risk of virtual team underperformance.

Note

Much of this information is excerpted from a workbook entitled *Managing Performance from a Distance* (The Fisher Group, Inc., 2010) that we use to train clients. Used by permission of the authors and copyright holders.

Chapter 15

Effective Decision Making over Distance

Gettin' good players is easy. Gettin' 'em to play together is the hard part.

—Casey Stengel

Making decisions in an effective and efficient manner is another critical skill for virtual teams to acquire. *Decision making* is the skill that allows teams to transform ideas into specific, agreed-upon actions. But making decisions in a group is more difficult than making decisions as an individual. And making them as a virtual team takes more work than making them as a collocated one. In this chapter we review common decision-making methods and suggest how to optimize them for virtual teams.

Decision-Making Challenges

There are some real benefits to effective virtual team decision making, but there are some real challenges, as well. These challenges include:

1. **Being timely:** Most organizations have deadlines and must make decisions quickly. Moreover, as competition continues to increase, so will the pressure to make decisions and act on them rapidly.

2. **Being high quality:** In today's work environment, doing things right the first time makes a big difference in effectiveness. In many cases, there's no second chance. Therefore, decisions must be accurate, precise, and well thought out.

3. **Fostering commitment in others:** The most accurate decision in the world is of little value if no one is willing to support and implement it. This is the essence of commitment. Often, even a mediocre decision that is supported with commitment can produce greater results than a good decision without commitment to implement.

Common Decision-Making Methods

Organizations use a variety of methods for making decisions. Some of the more common methods include autocratic, democratic, consensus, and unanimous decision making.

Autocratic Decision Making

The decision is made by one individual. This individual is often the person in charge, the manager or supervisor. This individual could also be a technical expert.

Democratic Decision Making

Also known as majority rule, the democratic method of decision making is common. Voting is normally used to determine the most popular decision. The alternative with the most votes wins. Many Web conferencing platforms have easy ways to facilitate this kind of decision making.

Consensus Decision Making

Consensus decision making occurs when all team members are committed to support the decision that has been made. Consensus does not mean that all the team members agree that this is the best possible decision—but *they will support the decision* reached and do not feel they are compromising their ethics, values, or interests in doing so.

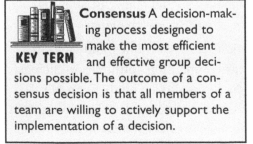

KEY TERM **Consensus** A decision-making process designed to make the most efficient and effective group decisions possible. The outcome of a consensus decision is that all members of a team are willing to actively support the implementation of a decision.

Unanimous Decision Making

Unanimous decision making means that everyone agrees the best possible decision has been made.

Why Virtual Teams Usually Use Consensus

Depending on the situation, different decision-making methodologies work better than others. In a technical situation where there is only one right answer, for example, an autocratic approach with a single individual taking charge is usually the most effective. This is also true of emergencies. The single decision maker doesn't have to be the virtual team leader, however. It could be the person with the most knowledge. Democratic decisions are useful when the support of the minority (the "losers" of the vote) isn't crtical. Unanimity is desirable if there is a mission-critical decision, and you have sufficient time to make everyone feel that the best possible decision was reached.

Generally, most situations faced by virtual work teams are neither one with only one correct answer nor emergencies requiring split-second response. Nor are they issues that can afford significan minority resistance, days of deliberation, or unanimous consent. In fact, the types of decisions most often faced by virtual work teams can best be made by using consensus (for a comparison of consensus and unanimous decision making, see Figure 15-1). Research has shown that decisions made by consensus tend to be faster (if you include implementation time), of better quality (the result of the variety of perspectives that are shared among group members during the decision-making process), and easier to implement (by definition, when consensus has been reached everyone has agreed to support it).

Consensus	Unanimous
■ Does not necessarily mean that every member of the group thinks the best possible decision has been made. ■ No one is morally, ethically, or professionally violated by the decision. ■ Every member of the group will actively support the decision	■ Everyone agrees that the best possible decision has been made.

Figure 15-1. Consensus versus unanimous decision making

Thus, consensus is most likely to overcome the three key challenges of decision making mentioned at the beginning of the chapter than the other methods.

Reaching Consensus as a Virtual Team

Consensus decision making is a method that requires the dedicated involvement of all team members. For a group to reach a consensus decision, three basic conditions must be met. First, everyone feels that he or she has had an opportunity to express an opinion. Second, no one in the group feels morally, ethically, or professionally violated by the decision. Third, every member of the group will support the decision after the meeting. This does not necessarily mean that every member of the group thinks the best possible decision has been made, but it does mean that every member is willing to *actively support* the decision. If any of these three conditions are not met, then a consensus decision has not been reached and more discussion by the group's membership is required.

When people are separated by space, time, or culture, nothing draws them together like working through a difficult decision. It's often messy, and usually requires compromise and patience, but at the end of the

SMART

MANAGING

USING CONSENSUS

Using consensus in virtual teams requires strict conformance to the three key rules: (1) Everyone has an opportunity to express an opinion. (2) No one feels professionally or ethically violated by the decision. (3) Everyone is willing to actively support it.

How do you know if the rules are followed? You have to ask. Every time. In new teams, or teams with new members, you would ask at the end of the meeting (assuming a teleconference), "Is there anyone else who wants to share an opinion before we make a decision?"

Then you would state the decision (doing the best you can to capture the emerging consensus that surfaced in the discussion) and ask, "Is there anyone who cannot actively support this decision for any reason?" As the team becomes more experienced, you may be able to use shorthand and simply ask, "Do we have consensus?" Remember that if even one person cannot actively support the decision, you do not have consensus. Either the discussion must continue until that person has a change of mind, or you must announce that you were unable to reach consensus and that you must use a different method.

process all the team members agree to implement a decision *that they made together*. It makes them feel like they belong to something bigger than themselves, and it reinforces the feeling of identity that is so important to people who have only infrequent opportunities to see each other face-to-face.

The Consensus Process

Many groups talk of using consensus decision making, and yet, when they are having difficulty reaching agreement, they resort to voting or rely on some identified "expert" to make the final decision. While these methods may become necessary as an alternative to consensus, they should not be confused with the consensus method.

The following steps are helpful when reaching consensus as a team.

1. **Clearly define the issue.** It's common sense that a good decision cannot be made if the issue being decided has not been clearly defined and is not widely understood by the group's membership. Unfortunately, groups often make decisions without clearly defining just what the issue or problem is they are trying to address. Often, by merely defining the issue, the best means to address it becomes obvious.

2. **Agree on a back-up process in case the team can't reach consensus.** As previously stated, consensus offers the best of all worlds when attempting to make team decisions that are timely, are of high quality, and that have the commitment of those who must implement them. However, there are occasions when a team simply cannot, for any number of reasons, reach consensus. For this reason, it's helpful for the group to agree on what alternative process will be used in the event the team does get in a bind and cannot close the decision. Will the team defer to a manager? Will a subteam be selected to go off and come up with a decision? Will the group vote?

   If a team finds itself frequently giving up on consensus, this is probably a sign of impatience or lack of practice. Deferring to managers, voting, and other methods won't provide the same benefits that come from consensus. It's better for the group to continue to struggle with the issue and explore new alternatives until a consensus can be reached.

3. **Gather information.** This may require postponing the decision long enough to get the information needed to consider all angles.

4. **Prepare your own thoughts regarding the issue.** All members of the group share the responsibility to prepare for the team discussion.

5. **Listen to the views of others on the team.** Allow others to fully express their views and try to understand their perspective.

6. **Share your thoughts with the group.** Just as all those involved in the decision share the responsibility of preparing for the discussion, it's also the responsibility of each member to express his or her thoughts and feelings with the group. As the manager, don't withhold your opinion. But be careful not to unduly influence the decision, either.

7. **Understand the similarities between positions.** Often, the temptation is to focus on the differences between viewpoints among group members rather than on their similarities. When trying to reach a consensus decision, it's important to define the common ground. This helps the group move toward making a decision on the points where general agreement already exists.

8. **Provide time and opportunity for viewpoints to be expressed.** It's important for all the team members to feel they have had ample opportunity to state their case. Dictating decisions weakens the entire team. People begin to feel that it really doesn't matter what they say because the decision has already been made. To assure that everyone has had a chance to speak, it's often helpful to ask each member of the group for any additional comments before the decision is made. This gives each member of the team a final chance to voice his or her views and can be helpful in certain cultures where people are reluctant to voice their opinions unless asked to do so.

9. **Make a decision as a team.** Reaching consensus as a team requires that you concentrate on reaching a decision that everyone can support, and not one merely based on your own preferences as the leader of the virtual team.

10. **Implement and support the decision as a team.** Once made, the entire team must take ownership for the decision and do everything possible to see that it is successfully implemented. That is what it means to "actively support" a decision. Passively allowing a decision

to proceed without resisting it is not acceptable.

Times When Consensus Does Not Work

There may be times when your team is having difficulty reaching consensus. Although this is common, it can still be frustrating to the team. Consider the following checklist to determine what is preventing your team from reaching consensus:

DECISION CONFUSION

The most common error new teams make is to confuse consensus with unanimous decision making. In consensus, having people willing to actively support the decision is sufficient. Don't keep talking until everyone feels you have reached the best possible decision unless you need to make a unanimous decision. This lengthens the process considerably, and is a luxury most virtual teams can ill afford.

THINGS TO TEACH VIRTUAL TEAM MEMBERS ABOUT CONSENSUS

SMART

MANAGING

- *Be prepared to discuss the issues.* Do your homework and be prepared to explain your position. If everyone does this, the best decision is easier to make.
- *Stay focused on the purpose of the decision.* It is easy to let the discussion get off track. Side discussions only confuse the decision-making process.
- *Say what is on your mind and take responsibility for being heard.* Speaking up is an important responsibility of each team member.
- *Listen so that you understand others.* Listening is critical to consensus decision making. Each team member must listen to the other in order to reach consensus.
- *Consider differing opinions as helpful to making a quality decision.* The objective is to make a quality decision. Differing points can add to the quality.
- *Avoid the urge to wrap things up too soon.* Make sure that everyone has been heard and that all points have been considered.
- *Don't be afraid to address conflict.* Conflict can help assure that a quality decision is reached. Make sure, however, that the conflict is centered on the issues at hand and not on the people involved.
- *Confront ideas and issues, not people.* It is worth saying again. Keep the discussion focused on the issues.
- *Work for a quality decision and not just your preferred choice.* This requires that team members be flexible and open to new ideas.
- *Agree to the final decision only if you feel you can fully support it.* Be honest

about what you think. If you know you will not support a decision, don't
pretend you will.
- *Keep an open mind and heart.* What you think and feel are important not
  only to the quality of a decision, but also to the quality of the implementation.

- Have we clearly defined the issue? Do we know what it is we are try-
  ing to decide?
- Are we the right group to be making this decision?
- Do we have all the information we need to make the decision?
- Are we each committed to make the decision by consensus?

METHODS FOR MAKING CONSENSUS DECISIONS ACROSS DISTANCE

TOOLS

When making a consensus decision in virtual teams, it is often
useful to have a simple method for quickly determining each
team member's position on the decision being discussed. If you
are using cameras, try this:

1. State the proposed decision.
2. Ask people to each show a sign signifying their position on the proposal
   as follows:
   - A thumbs-up sign means "I fully support the proposal."
   - A thumbs-to-the-side sign means "This isn't my favorite idea but I am
     willing to support it."
   - A thumbs-down sign means "I will not support this decision."
3. Ask the people who display a thumbs-down sign to share their concerns.
4. After everyone has had an opportunity to express his or her views fully,
   modify the proposal if necessary or call for people to resignify their
   position on the original proposal.
5. If everyone now has a thumb-to-the-side or thumbs-up, *congratulations*—you have consensus. If you still have some thumbs-down, continue the discussion or agree that you cannot reach consensus and must
   choose another method.

If you are not using cameras or the cultures you work with find the
thumbs method distasteful, an alternative approach is to give participants
the opportunity to say "green light" if they think the best possible decision
has been suggested, "yellow light" if they are willing to actively support the
decision but it isn't their favorite one, or "red light" if they cannot support
the decision.

- Are we being totally honest with our feelings and motives?
- Are there issues related to this decision that we haven't discussed?
- Are we taking the decision too seriously or too lightly?
- Do we agree on what "active support" of the decision means?

Ultimately, although consensus decision making is fairly easy to understand conceptually, it takes a great deal of practice to master it as a virtual team. But if you do, you will find the most efficient and effective process available for creating timely, high-quality decisions, with the maximum support possible for the time invested.

Manager's Checklist for Chapter 15

☑ There are four common methods for making decisions in virtual teams. They are.

1. Autocratic decisions made by one person
2. Democratic (or majority rules) voting
3. Consensus (where people are willing to actively support a decision even if it is not their first choice)
4. Unanimous decisions (where everyone agrees that the best possible decision has been made)

☑ Research indicates that consensus decisions are generally the most efficient and effective method of the group decision-making options. It is also a powerful way for virtual teams to pull together and create a shared identity.

☑ The three key rules for consensus are, first, everyone must have an opportunity to express an opinion; second, no one can feel morally, ethically, or professionally violated by the decision; and third, everyone actively supports the decision. If even one person feels one of the rules has been broken, you do not have a consensus.

☑ The recommended steps for all team members to follow together to make a consensus decision-making process include:

1. Clearly define the issue.
2. Agree on a back-up process in case the team can't reach consensus.
3. Gather information.
4. Prepare your own thoughts regarding the issue.

5. Listen to the views of others on the team.

6. Share your thoughts with the group.

7. Understand the similarities between positions.

8. Provide time and opportunity for viewpoints to be expressed.

9. Make a decision as a team.

10. Implement and support the decision as a team.

☑ There are times when consensus decision making is not appropriate and another method should be used. These include emergency situations, decisions where there is one right answer known only by a technical expert, and decisions where team input will not be considered.

☑ The most common error for new virtual teams is to confuse consensus with unanimous decision making. You do not need to have everyone on the team feel that the best possible decision has been made. You only need everyone to actively support it.

☑ To ensure consensus, the virtual team manager (or meeting facilitator) must either use a method (such as the thumbs or traffic light method) or ask if she or he must ask if each team member can actively support the decision. You can never assume that silence is agreement.

Note

Much of this information is excerpted from a workbook entitled *Effective Decision Making* (The Fisher Group, Inc., 2010). Used by permission of the authors and copyright holders.

Chapter
16

Virtual Team Building

No member of a crew is praised for the rugged individuality of his rowing.

—Ralph Waldo Emerson

Team building is an important way to rejuvenate and improve teams. Done properly, it can build or restore trust, create better work relationships, and improve general team effectiveness. In this chapter we review a number of virtual team-building methodologies in more detail and share tips on how to make virtual team-building activities more productive.

Two Types of Team Building

There are two types of team building activities: The first focuses on improving relationships, and the second focuses on improving the team's ability to perform its tasks. Although some team-building activities incorporate elements of both relationship and task improvement, most exercises emphasize one more than another. Generally, both types of team building are important for people to work together effectively.

Relationship Team Building

Relationship team building is important to foster trust and cooperation. This type of team building is especially helpful when new teams are formed (e.g., when project teams are commissioned, during meetings or

KEY TERMS

Relationship **team building** Helps people build social or interpersonal skills.

Task-effectiveness **team building** Helps people build technical or business skills.

training sessions with relative strangers, when new employees come on board, or when short temporary assignments require collaboration with people outside the normal work group). Relationship team building is also important when team effectiveness has eroded.

Relationship team building begins with activities that help us get to know each other better. Basic relationship team building can be used in early team meetings after a team has been formed, or as "ice-breaker" activities for training sessions or meetings with people who don't normally work together. They are also important to help with a refocusing or re-tasking initiative.

Task-Effectiveness Team Building

Task-effectiveness team building is important to help people be more productive. It is normally focused on identifying and eliminating barriers to performance (e.g., to improve quality, streamline workflow processes, reduce cost, etc.). These activities focus less on improving relationships and more on improving work processes.

CAUTION

TAKE CARE IN TEAM BUILDING

A team-building activity that works well with one team may be a disaster for another. Be sensitive to whether team members are comfortable with an activity, and be prepared to substitute another exercise if necessary. Some team-building activities, for example, call for a level of disclosure or trust that may make some people uncomfortable in particular cultures, and may be counterproductive if forced on unwilling participants.

Assessing Virtual Team Effectiveness

Before we discuss a few team-building activities, we would like to review a tool for helping virtual teams determine their effectiveness. This tool is excerpted from a Fisher Group assessment entitled "Assessing Virtual Team Effectiveness." Use it to determine what areas may require training and development interventions, including things like team-building activities, mentoring or coaching projects, or workshops and Webinars.

Virtual Team Effectiveness Assessment

To what extent is each statement an accurate description of the team you are assessing (low, medium, high)?

1. Our team meets synchronously on a regular basis (e.g., teleconference, videoconference, Web conference, etc.).
2. We have several methods for communicating with each other asynchronously (e.g., e-mail, voice mail, etc.).
3. Project deadlines and commitments are met by all team members.
4. The team meets financial goals.
5. Team members have access to all the information, tools, and other resources needed to do their work.
6. The team's output is high and of good quality.
7. The team is effective at solving problems and has a number of problem-solving tools at its disposal.
8. The team selects the right virtual technologies for its tasks.
9. The team meets face-to-face when necessary or at regularly scheduled intervals.
10. All team members are trained and competent in the virtual communication technologies they use (i.e., e-mail, voice mail, Web conferencing, teleconferencing, instant messaging, videoconferencing, etc.).
11. The team has established technology-use protocols and adheres to them.
12. Teleconferences are well organized and effective.
13. Web conferences are well structured and productive.
14. During Web conferences, techniques are used to keep participants highly engaged.
15. Clear goals and measures of performance are established and understood by all team members.
16. Each team member understands how his or her individual goals fit into the larger picture and help the team achieve its goals.
17. Roles and responsibilities of team members are clearly defined and understood.
18. The team has a clearly defined charter.
19. The team has a mutually agreed-on set of operating guidelines to manage its interactions.
20. All team members adhere to the established set of operating guidelines.
21. Methods for giving feedback to one another are established and used regularly by all team members.
22. The team has a defined and effective process for selecting new team members.

23. The team has a well-defined orientation process for new team members.
24. When a new team member comes on board, team members take time to conduct an in-depth, synchronous introduction of him or her to other team members.
25. Team members are well prepared to work across the different cultures represented on the team.
26. The quality of the team's decisions is high.
27. When collaborating on projects, team members regularly send each other status reports pertaining to their specific tasks.

Assessment Results

Once you have a feel for the relative strengths and weaknesses of your team, choose appropriate team-building interventions. If some of the indicators of team collaboration are low, for example, you might choose a relationship team-building activity that makes people more comfortable with one another. As we mentioned in earlier chapters, it is difficult to interact (and trust) people you don't know as human beings (not just as work nodes in your network). Conversely, if the opportunity is in the area of strengthening business or technical effectiveness, consider a task-effectiveness team-building activity.

FAMILIARITY WITH TECHNOLOGY MAY NOT ALWAYS BE A GOOD THING

While writing this chapter, one of the authors took a break to go out to lunch. Two teenage boys were in a booth nearby. They each had laptops set in front of them and were engaged in a virtual role-playing computer game. During the 30 minutes of observing the boys, the author noted only one short conversation lasting no more than 30 seconds between the friends. The good news for virtual teams is that this generation of workers will have little hesitation to interact virtually with other team members and will also have much higher skills in virtual communication. But will they know how to build relationships face-to-face?

A report on the NBC evening news with Brian Williams announced research that shows that 77 percent of 17-year-olds with a cell phone texted their friends daily, but that only 34 percent of them physically met their friends every day (NBC News, August 25, 2010). Is it any wonder that our clients report that many younger virtual team members have advanced communication technology skills, but lack some of the basic interpersonal skills that normally get developed over a history of face-to-face interactions?

Remember that any task-effectiveness intervention can be done in a way that builds skills *and* builds the team. Unfortunately, it is also true that you can conduct an activity in a way that destroys trust, creates conflict, and erodes team effectiveness. If, for example, you decide to do a team-building activity that will help

> **PAY ATTENTION TO STRENGTHS**
>
> TRICKS OF THE TRADE
>
> Smart managers know that you don't spend all your team-building time trying to improve team weaknesses. Sometimes the best intervention is to help a team strengthen something that it already excels at doing. A team that perfects its strengths almost always outperforms one that only shores up its weaknesses.

the team create operating guidelines or technology-use protocols, but you do it in a way that is perceived by the team as unnecessarily critical or demeaning, you may improve technical skills but diminish team effectiveness.

Road-Tested Team-Building Examples

Here are some sample team-building activities to help you improve your virtual team:

My Favorite Job (Relationship)

To get to know each other and to better understand how people like to work, each team member discusses the best job he or she ever had and why he or she liked it so much. It works best if you have people choose a job other than their current one. Write these comments down on a chart pad if you are in a face-to-face meeting, or put them on a whiteboard in a Webinar setting. After a few minutes, people will see that many of us value things like autonomy, meaningful work, variety, and respect from other team members. This insight often creates common ground among team members.

A variation of this exercise is to create an agreement about how the elements on the "my favorite job" list can be incorporated into the way this team will work together. To do this, try a multivoting technique (team members get five votes each to allocate as they wish—they can put all five on an item they feel strongly about, or they can split the votes). Then come to a consensus decision about how the items with the most votes can be incorporated into the way the team functions. Document this agreement.

Special Joint Activity (Relationship)

During face-to-face meetings, in particular, you can use special activities to build the team. Two of our favorites include making lunch and doing community service. Since you have to eat anyway, why not take a little extra time to go shopping for food and then make your lunch or dinner together? Afterward you can discuss whether any behavioral patterns surfaced that are either exemplary or atypical of the way the team works together. You might hear something like, "Maria is always so willing to help everybody. We should all be more like that" or "Don really took charge. He does that a lot. Sometimes that helps our team, but sometimes it prevents others from making important contributions."

Community service can be a wonderful way to build a team and do something good at the same time. Our clients at Weyerhaeuser, for example, often use the evenings of their face-to-face meeting times to help Habitat for Humanity build homes for the less fortunate. This is especially meaningful to the Weyerhaeuser team members who make dimensional lumber and can get personal experience working shoulder-to-shoulder with their teammates, using their own products, to help other people.

Two Truths and a Lie (Relationship)

A fun way to get to know more about one another is to have each team member share two things about themselves that are true and one that is not. After each person makes his or her presentation, the team then guesses which of the three statements is a lie. Expect a lot of laughter if you do this one correctly. Although you can do this one on a teleconference, it is more fun if you have a video component that allows everyone to see one another's expressions.

Sociogram (Relationship)

Using a sociogram analysis can be a powerful team-building experience. The sociogram is a way to graphically document team interactions during a meeting and discuss whether they are healthy or not.

Here's how it works: Draw a circle on a chartpad if you are in a face-to-face meeting, or use the whiteboard feature of a Web meeting tool if you are on a Web conference (this tool can also be used by the manager to privately document what happens on a teleconference). The circle represents the

> **Sociogram** A team analysis tool that displays team interactions.
>
> **KEY TERM**

team. Around the edges of the team circle, draw a smaller circle for each member of the team and label it accordingly (see Figure 16-1). The way you use our version of this tool is then to draw a circle in the middle and label it "All." Each time someone on the team speaks during the meeting you make a mark on the diagram. The first time the person speaks, draw an arrow from the person speaking to the person being addressed. If the comment is not directed to any person in particular, draw the arrow to the circle labeled "All." For any subsequent interaction to the same person or persons, draw a hash line on the arrow. In the Figure 16-1, for example, Bob spoke to everyone ("All") three times, to Mei twice, and to Kathy three times. The only person who spoke directly to him was Carlos.

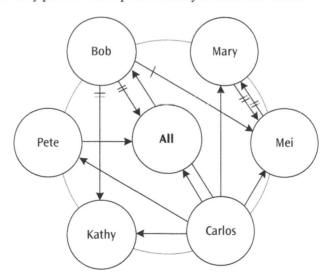

Figure 16-1. The sociogram

At the end of the meeting, show the completed diagram to the team and ask questions such as:

- What are the patterns we can see in the sociogram? Are these patterns typical?

■ Do we have cliques in our team?

■ Are some people regularly left out of our conversations?

■ Do some people interact more often with certain people than others? Why?

■ What does the sociogram show about who are the informal leaders in the team?

■ Do we ever have problems with some people dominating discussions?

■ Are certain people ignored or overlooked during some discussions?

■ Do our interactions change depending on the topic we're discussing? How? Why?

■ Do we have dynamics that are gender-, job-, race-, age-, or education-related? How does that affect us?

In the sample sociogram, we would also probably ask:

■ Does it mean anything that Carlos spoke to several people, but no one spoke to him?

■ Should we be concerned that Kathy didn't make a single comment?

■ Does it matter that Mary and Mei spoke together six times but never addressed anyone else?

Chartering (Task-Effectiveness)

Few things are as potentially powerful for a task-effectiveness team-building activity as a discussion about team purpose. For this exercise, have each virtual team member come prepared with a three-to-five-word phrase that captures the primary reason for the team's existence. After each person shares his or her statement, look first for commonalities and then for critical areas of disagreement that must be resolved. At the conclusion of the meeting, ask for a volunteer to write a brief team charter that incorporates the agreements into a single statement. At the next virtual team meeting, wordsmith and finalize the statement. Consider having team members affix their signatures to the charter and then post it on your Web site or wiki.

Voice of the Customer (Task-Effectiveness)

Invite a key customer or stakeholder to join a virtual team meeting and share something he or she really likes about the team, and something he or she would like to have the team do differently. If done properly, this conversation can both have a celebratory feel (all teams like to be winners) and provide an opportunity for improvement. It is often more powerful to have this information come from the customer in person than to hear it from you as the manager.

In conclusion, remember that virtual teams normally require more team-building activities than collocated teams. Working together face-to-face routinely is a type of task and relationship-oriented team-building effort in and of itself.

Manager's Checklist for Chapter 16

☑ Activities such as the voice of the customer, chartering, making lunch or doing service work together, sociogram diagramming and analysis, two truths and a lie, and my favorite job are good examples of how team-building exercises can strengthen your virtual team.

☑ Before conducting a virtual team-building exercise, conduct a team effectiveness assessment to help you decide which activity will most benefit your team. This type of assessment can guide other skill-building interventions, such as mentoring and coaching activities or formal training workshops.

☑ Team-building activities can be separated into two categories. Relationship team building serves to build relationships and personal trust, while task-effectiveness team building works on improving the delivery mechanisms for working together to accomplish a shared task.

Note

Much of this information is excerpted from an assessment called *Assessing Virtual Team Effectiveness* (The Fisher Group, Inc., 2010) and a workbook entitled *Team-Building* (The Fisher Group, Inc., 2010). Used by permission of the authors and copyright holders.

Chapter
17

Maintaining a Balanced Personal and Work Life

This is perhaps the most beautiful time in human history; it is really pregnant with all kinds of creative possibilities made possible by science and technology which now constitute the slave of man—if man is not enslaved by it.

—Jonas Salk

In the final chapter of this book, we'd like to discuss a difficult problem. In a communication technology–enabled world, how do you disconnect? How can you (as a virtual team leader) maintain balance in your work and personal life? How can you help your team members do the same? When we ask this question in our workshops, we notice a lot of people frowning and looking at their feet. Once, a manager (with small children) asked hopefully, "Is that possible?"

Our answer is that it is not only possible, but desirable. It is not, however, easy. We make several recommendations we hope will help you strike this balance, but first we'd like to put this issue into context. Therefore, after a few examples to illustrate the problem, we open the chapter with a discussion of organizational design that will, we hope, illustrate why a healthy personal life should be on the agenda of every virtual team leader.

The Work and Home Life Balance Problem

Several years ago, in an interesting segment on the popular weekly news television program *60 Minutes*, reporter Leslie Stahl discussed an alarming pattern of people who work such long hours that their personal lives suffer significantly (Leslie Stahl, "Working 24/7," *60 Minutes* [Television broadcast], CBS News, 2006). It wasn't so much a program about workaholism—a personal choice about addiction to work that some managers have made for decades—as it was a program about how communication technologies intrude into every area of a virtual team leader's life. She joked that many of the people who used to work 9–5 now work 5–9 because technologies promote it.

Some of the vignettes she showed included a virtual team member who regularly worked from home until midnight and another who got up very early to jog to an Internet café to teleconference into a daily virtual team meeting. She interviewed a manager who had an Internet connection installed in his shower so as never to be out of touch with his virtual team, and a busy couple who used technology so much (and were so tired from doing things like getting up at 3 A.M. to check e-mails and make international calls) that they often found themselves sitting next to each other on the couch texting each other as a substitute for a conversation. Not surprisingly, their baby's favorite toy was a Blackberry. One humorous (and also sad) video showed a father on his day off trying unsuccessfully to play with his children while on a work teleconference.

Modern technology no longer allows a separation from home and work, and many people find that their relationships, volunteering and service opportunities, and personal health suffer as a result. In some cases, our interpersonal skills may actually diminish from disuse.

Should we be concerned about a balanced life? We think so. If personal effectiveness erodes because a healthy home and work life balance cannot be maintained, neither the individual nor the organization benefits. In the *60 Minutes* news report mentioned above, for example, costly stress-related health claims from employees at Best Buy were the primary reason it decided to make some important changes in its work culture. After not requiring people to go to the office unless their work demanded it (many people now work of lot of time at home) and instituting a "results only" work culture (they no longer track work hours, for example, only whether the assigned projects are completed appropriately), stress decreased and results improved.

But unfortunately, many organizations have difficulty even having this kind of conversation. Talking about what happens at home, for example, is avoided. That discussion is often deemed either "none of our business" or irrelevant, largely as a result of the bias of a long organizational history of work design that has ignored whatever happens outside of work. We can't do that any longer. Consider a brief history of how team-based operations have typically been organized.

A Brief History of Organizational Design

Many people consider Eric Trist, Fred Emery, and their colleagues at the Tavistock Institute in post–World War II England as the fathers of the modern team concept. Among their many contributions to the field, Trist and Emery suggested that the design of teams should consider both the social and the technical aspects of work. Justifiably criticizing several early organization design efforts as emphasizing either the social system ("We'll pipe nice music into the office and paint it pleasant colors, and people will be more productive even if we don't have good tools for them to use") or the technical system ("As long as we have the most modern equipment, we'll be more competitive, even if we don't take the time to train people how to use it"), they suggested that both the people structures and processes (social system) and the tools and business systems operated by them (technical system) needed to be "jointly optimized" (Fred Emery & Eric Trist, "Socio-technical systems," in C. Churchman & M. Verhuist [Eds.], *Management sciences models and techniques*, London: Pergamon Press, 1960). They thereby created the sociotechnical systems (STS) perspective that still influences much of the current practice of team-based organizational design and is represented by the Venn diagram shown in Figure 17-1.

Subsequent research convinced STS practitioners that an essential part of the design equation was the business environment surrounding the team. Thus, the design process evolved to include what Emery and Trist called the "environmental scan," which was an essential way to incorporate the customer voice and competitive realities of the external marketplace place into team design (Eric Trist, *The evolution of socio-technical systems: A conceptual framework and an action research program*, Ontario

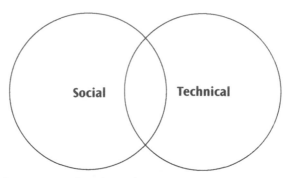

Figure 17-1. The social and technical systems

Quality of Working Life Centre, 1981). Now teams were designed to jointly optimize the social and technical systems in a way that responded to real business pressures and often resulted in real business gains. This is represented by Figure 17-2.

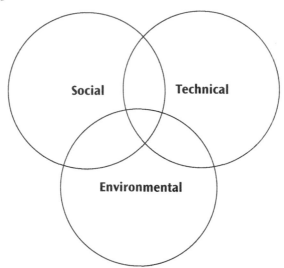

Figure 17-2. The social, technical, and environmental systems

With the rapid growth of virtual teams, however, the design process needs to incorporate one additional system: the personal system. Although past design processes have often acknowledged that work design affects home life, virtual team design makes the boundary between work and personal life more permeable. Virtual team members often work at least part of their time from home. Furthermore, members of virtual global teams are frequently required to participate in team tele-conferences or Web conferences from home because they are conducted outside normal working hours to accommodate team members who live in different time zones. Perhaps most important, we live in a time blessed and cursed by new communication technologies: blessed because the work of virtual teams would be almost impossible without these new technologies, but cursed because virtual team members are forever teth-ered to work. For many team members, a certain amount of work, such as checking e-mail or voice mail, is normally done at home.

The Technology Tether

When your workplace is cyberspace, it follows you wherever you go. When we recently asked what his primary concern was for members of the virtual teams in his organization, the president of Cummins Power Generation declared, "Home and work life balance!" instead of the plethora of motivation and coordination concerns we thought he would mention. There are good reasons for this. Many people average three hours of e-mail a day, much of it read at home to allow office time to be maximized (Leslie Stahl, "Working 24/7," *60 Minutes* [Television broad-cast], CBS News, 2006). We found an even more startling statistic in a study we conducted in which members of a virtual sales team spent an average of six hours a day doing e-mail—most of it from home to allow for as much face-to-face time with customers as possible.

The Personal System

Organizational designers and senior managers have traditionally been understandably reluctant to intrude into the previously off-limits terri-tory of team members' personal lives when engaging in design or start-up activities. This justifiable concern acknowledges the importance of people's ability to maintain private lives and to ensure the protection of their personal rights and security. Ironically, the lack of these discussions in new virtual teams leads to further encroachment into the personal space by unrestrained work demands.

The use of operating guidelines and technology-use protocols (men-tioned earlier in the book) allows people to reestablish the appropriate boundaries between work and personal life that have been eroded by pervasive technologies. When this is done effectively, many clients report this improves organizational productivity while reducing personal stress and health problems. By jointly optimizing all four systems (see Figure 17-3 for a representation of the social, technical, environmental, and personal systems—or what we call our STEP systems design model), we can now design for the whole human organizational system, a goal referenced, but unachievable, by many of the organization systems design methodologies of the past.

SMART MANAGING

TIPS FOR CREATING BALANCE

Here are some tips the managers we interviewed suggested for improving personal and work life balance. These may not work for everyone, but they do illustrate the different approaches managers take to addressing this challenge:

- Reserve a regular time each week (when you're in town) for family or friends (e.g., Fridays are date night, or Wednesday night is basketball).
- Discuss times for special events with the members of your team, so they'll know when you can't be available for meetings (and in some cases can celebrate or mourn with you), due to weddings, childbirths, funerals, etc.
- Find a way to stay in touch when you are traveling (for example, make a videophone call to your kids each night).
- When possible, involve your friends and family in appropriate work-related activities (e.g., take advantage of the "bring your daughter to work day" even if you work remotely from home).
- Make and keep medical appointments. Do the suggested regular checkups. Take your medicine.
- Exercise regularly.
- Eat like you know you should.
- Schedule time to volunteer in your community. It won't happen unless you make it happen.

Other evidence validates the need for balance. In the Cummins Power Generation business, many of the best-adjusted and most effective virtual team leaders had discovered that they needed to put some personal interaction boundaries in place to maintain their private lives and stay healthy. But these boundaries often required support from other members of the virtual team and therefore required discussion with them. One leader, for

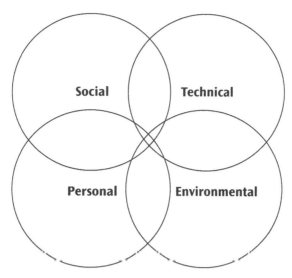

Figure 17-3. The social, technical, environmental, and personal (step) systems

example, contracted with his team to reply to evening e-mails quickly, but requested that on the days he was in town he have two hours each evening to have dinner with his wife and put his children to bed. The team members readily agreed. He probably now works later into the night than he would have otherwise, but says he is happier and healthier as a result.

YOU (NOT THE ORGANIZATION) ARE RESPONSIBLE FOR BALANCE

TRICKS OF THE TRADE

Although a number of organizations have tried to do things to help virtual team members achieve a balance between their personal and work life (parts of IBM, for example, have instituted ThinkFridays, a day on which no meetings are supposed to be held), ultimately only you can establish the proper balance. This often requires a new openness about your personal life ("My daughter is getting married next week and I won't be available on Thursday") that might have been seen as inappropriate before.

Some leaders also put, for example, personal information on their shared work calendar (Dental appointment next Wednesday). Others have discussions about accommodations with their teams ("I'm reserving Monday nights for my family"). Still others find it necessary to negotiate with their company about more realistic expectations about work hours. But don't expect your team or organization to ask you how they can help you. You'll have to take responsibility for managing your life.

Tips for Working at Home

Virtual team managers often work at least part of their time from home. This can be challenging if you don't live alone. The managers we interviewed suggested the following tips for you (and/or the people you lead remotely):

Try to find a way to provide a physical separation between your work space and the rest of your home. A room with a door is ideal. Shutting the door can signal to your family or roommates that you shouldn't be disturbed for anything less than an emergency, and perhaps even more important, it provides a psychological barrier between home and work. Close the door at the end of the workday to reduce your temptation to check e-mail or spend just a few more minutes on that pressing project. If you don't have a space with a door, consider getting something like a desk that can be shut up into a cabinet, so that you can close it at the end of the day.

Identify start and stop times for work. You'll have to be somewhat flexible on this depending on what happens on any given day, but it will help you to remember to take time to eat, exercise, and leave some personal time in your schedule. It also makes it easier to manage your relationships with other people in the home.

Discuss your situation with the people you live with. Figure out ways to identify times when you can't be interrupted, and times when you can. This is especially important for homes with children. It can be frustrating for kids to see Mom or Dad at home if they don't understand when it is OK to talk to them and when it isn't. A home with pets can also be problematic if you don't have a plan. There is nothing quite as distracting as a baying dog in the background right in the middle of that important call to your customer.

Remember that certain home situations aren't conducive to working. If the physical situation doesn't allow for it, or if the arrangement won't work with the people you live with, or you don't have the emotional ability or mental mindset to work productively from the same place where you eat and sleep, untenable problems will probably develop. Not everyone dreams of going to work in their bathrobe and slippers. Some people need to go to an office outside their home to be productive.

Make sure that you either know enough about your technologies to troubleshoot them yourself or have access to some good resources to help you when you have problems. It can be frustrating to lose your Internet connection in the middle of an important Web meeting. You'll probably also need to know whom you can talk to when you get stuck on a nontechnical problem. Can you ask your boss for suggestions when you are puzzled about a decision or need to bounce an idea off someone who understands your business? If not, whom can you call?

Many teams have discussions during the start-up—especially during the development of operating guidelines and technology protocols—that create cultural expectations about matters like whether projects require people to respond to work communications during vacation time and weekends, whether accommodations will be made for religious holidays that affect only a few team members, or whether participating in important family milestone activities or emergencies can be allowed during critical work periods. The way these discussions are handled can affect the trust of the team and either promote or diminish virtual team effectiveness.

Managing a virtual team can be a difficult job. But it can also be rewarding. Managing the balance between your work life and personal life is one of the keys to a long, healthy, and successful career leading remote employees. If you can do that, you'll be better prepared to withstand the rigors of a challenging career with increasing responsibilities for larger and larger groups of more distributed workers. But a balanced life will prepare you for something even more important than successful career advancement. There are few people who lie on their deathbed and wish they had spent more time at work. Many lament the lost opportunities with loved ones. If you want a happier life, don't be one of those people.

Manager's Checklist for Chapter 17

☑ Make the commitments and changes required to keep an appropriate balance between your work and personal life.

☑ Use operating guidelines and technology-use protocol discussions to negotiate family-friendly/personal life-friendly communication practices.

☑ Talk (appropriately) about your personal life. Put major events on the shared calendar.

☑ Be healthy. Take care of yourself. Only you can do it.

☑ Just because organizations have a long history of staying out of our individual lives doesn't mean we have to continue that pattern. With advances in technology that make us available 24/7, we have to take extraordinary measures to maintain personal balance. Smart executives understand that appropriate interventions not only help people do their work at home more effectively, but can also help them find the time to take care of their health and their loved ones and improve their communities. Balanced employees are more likely to be productive over the long term, present a more desirable face of the corporation in their towns, and demonstrate loyalty to employers. Besides, it's just the right thing to do.

Note

Much of this information comes from a chapter Kimball wrote in *The Virtual Handbook of High Performance Virtual Teams* (Kimball Fisher, "Tools for Effective Virtual Team Start-Ups," San Francisco: Jossey-Bass, 2008), which excerpts material from two workbooks we use to train clients including *Virtual Team Start-Ups* (The Fisher Group, Inc., 2006) and *Using Communication Technologies Effectively* (The Fisher Group, Inc., 2010). Used by permission of the authors and copyright holders.

Index

About the Authors

Kimball Fisher and Mareen Duncan Fisher are co-founders of The Fisher Group, Inc. (**www.thefishergroup.com**), a workplace learning company that specializes in training programs for managers and work teams. Their clients include about 1/4th of the *Fortune* 100 (companies such as Apple, Bristol-Myers Squibb, Chevron, General Dynamics, Hewlett-Packard, Intel, McDonald's Corp., Microsoft, NBC [General Electric], Nike, Tropicana [PepsiCo], and WellPoint) and public organizations such as the U.S. Department of Treasury and the Staff Office of The U.S. Senate, as well as smaller corporations, universities, and not-for-profit organizations. They have traveled to more than 30 countries and have worked with clients across North America, Europe, Scandinavia, Asia, South Africa and Mexico.

The Fishers are the best-selling authors of *The Distance Manager, Leading Self-Directed Work Teams*, and *The Distributed Mind*, as well as numerous professional articles, DVDs, and book chapters on the topics of leadership and teams. They are frequent keynote speakers, Webinar leaders, and guest lecturers. Kimball was the first recipient of the prestigious William G. Dyer award for significant contributions to the field of organizational behavior and Mareen is an honored member of the International Who's Who of Entrepreneurs. Both have been designated *Thought Leaders* by the Drucker Foundation and received their Master of Organizational Behavior degrees from Brigham Young University. Prior to consulting, the Fishers worked for Procter & Gamble and Tektronix. Mareen also worked for Weyerhaeuser. Their work has been noted for its pragmatic, results-oriented style, influenced by their personal experience as successful work team leaders.